12- A.
26- A.

1990

VETERAN CARS

In the Same Series:

VETERAN CARS

ERNEST F. CARTER

1914 Delaunay-Relleville

Burke Books **B** LONDON & TORONTO

First published 1959
Reprinted September 1960
Revised and reprinted May 1972

© Burke Publishing Company Limited 1959 and 1972

ISBN 0 222 69702 4

Burke Publishing Company Limited
14 John Street, London, WC1N 2EJ
Burke Publishing (Canada) Limited
73 Six Point Road, Toronto 18, Ontario

Printed in Great Britain
by The Anchor Press Ltd.,
and bound by Wm. Brendon & Son Ltd.,
both of Tiptree, Essex

ACKNOWLEDGMENTS

The author and publishers wish to thank the following for permission to reproduce illustrations:

A.C. Motors Ltd.; *Autocar*; R. Boulton-Peacock, Esq.; British Motor Corporation; Brooks (Motor Components) Ltd.; The Director, The Science Museum, London; G. S. Finlayson, Esq.; Ford Motors; C. Landauer, Esq.; London County Council; Montagu Motor Museum

Contents

CHAPTER I

The First London-Brighton Run

TOWARDS THE end of the eighteenth century the necessity for the speedy conveyance of both passengers and merchandise came to be widely felt, had railways not appeared upon the scene at the beginning of the nineteenth century there is no doubt that some new form of power for speeding up transport would have been developed at a much earlier date than was actually the case.

As early as the year 1769 a French mechanic of Lorraine, Nicholas Joseph Cugnot, designed and constructed the first self-propelled road vehicle which actually carried passengers. It was a crude three-wheeled, steam-driven affair which travelled at 2¼ m.p.h. Unluckily, it overturned at a Paris street corner, with the result that both invention and inventor were impounded by the police! Cugnot, however, was soon released and his road locomotive may still be seen at the Paris *Conservatoire des Arts et Métiers*.

There is not room in this book to do more than mention the very interesting vehicles used on the roads with success during the first half of the nineteenth century, when the initiative and foresight of such pioneers of steam road-coach construction were hampered and restricted in Britain by the ridiculous legislation of the Parliament of the day. This, too, was indirectly responsible for the fact that for many years Great Britain was a long way behind in the race for the supremacy of the motor industry.

Steam-driven Cars

Nor should we overlook the steam-driven road vehicles of the 1860s and 1870s; the Frenchman, Amedée Bollée, who in 1875 ran his steam carriage from Le Mans to Paris, a distance of 142 miles; Serpollet, Scotte, Le Blant, De Dion and Bouton, and the other Frenchmen, who successfully used steam in road carriages from 1887. It must be remembered that it was the successes of these early steam-driven machines which brought the possibilities of mechanical road traction before the general public just at the very time when the internal combustion engine was to appear with petroleum spirit as a fuel. This was the engine which was eventually to convince the civilised world that mechanically-driven road vehicles were not freaks, but practical machines capable of doing a real job of work.

The argument as to who built the first internal combustion motor car seems never to have been completely settled. In 1884 the German, Gottlieb Daimler, invented the first high-speed petrol engine, which he patented five years later. His fellow-countryman, Carl Benz, built his first motor car in 1885 and patented it the following year. The Daimler engine was taken up by the French firm of Panhard and Levassor. They applied it to road vehicles and developed a successful design the arrangement of which has been followed generally ever since. Benz's rather crude three-wheeled vehicle with its ¾-h.p. slow-speed engine and belt drive was not improved upon until his collaborator, August Horch, realising that the three-wheelers were under-powered, produced a better engine with greater horse-power which added five miles per hour to the speed of the vehicle.

one by one. He placed the engine vertically, in front of the car, inside a cover (bonnet) to keep out the dust from the roads of the day; he put the clutch in the engine flywheel; he fitted cog-wheels of varying ratios to allow a change of

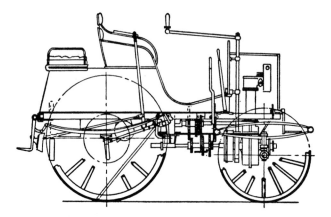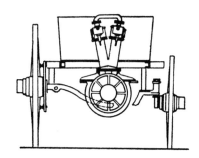

Panhard-Levassor car of 1894

Now the petrol motor car had become a practical proposition, instead of a universal laughing-stock, and the use of steam as a source of power looked like being superseded. The Daimler-engined Panhard-Levassor car of the early 1890s contained a sliding change-speed gear and clutch of Emile Levassor's own design which were substantially the same as those in use on the great majority of present-day motor cars; the engine of today, with the exception of its electrical ignition and mechanically-operated inlet valves, differs little from the original Daimler engine as Levassor adapted it to a motor car. Indeed, if a modern motor car is placed beside the original vehicle, it will be found that the car has preserved its original characteristics much more than the modern steam railway locomotive has preserved those of the "Rocket". The wonderful development of the automobile owes more to refinement than to novelty.

Levassor introduced his improvements

speed to be made; he introduced a countershaft with a differential gear to equalise the drive between the rear wheels; and he mounted the whole assembly on a stout wooden frame or chassis which rested on axles provided with springs.

The First Motor Race

Then, in 1894 (the same year in which one of these cars was brought to England by the Hon. Evelyn Ellis) the French newspaper, *Le Petit Journal*, organised a series of trials for mechanical road vehicles. This concluded with the celebrated 74½-mile Paris-Rouen race, which was held in July. The car which finished first was a De Dion Bouton steam tractor with a six-seater trailer attached. It covered the course in 4 hours 40 minutes, at an average speed of 12 m.p.h. Five minutes later, two Panhard-engined Peugeot four-seaters arrived, to be followed thirteen minutes later by a four-seater Panhard-Levassor.

Here is a complete list of the competing cars in this, the first motor car "race" of all time:

In the following year, 1895, the famous Paris-Bordeaux-Paris race of 745 miles was held in which Emile Levassor put up

			hrs.	mins.	Engine
De Dion Bouton .	Steam	6 seats	5	40	—
Peugeot . . .	Petrol	4 seats	5	45	3½-h.p. Daimler
Peugeot . . .	Petrol	4 seats	5	50	3½-h.p. Daimler
Panhard-Levassor .	Petrol	4 seats	6	3	3½-h.p. Daimler
Peugeot . . .	Petrol	5 seats	6	7	3½-h.p. Daimler
Le Brun . .	Petrol	4 seats	6	24	Le Brun
Panhard-Levassor .	Petrol	2 seats	6	30	3½-h.p. Daimler
Panhard-Levassor .	Petrol	4 seats	6	49	3½-h.p. Daimler
De Bourmont . .	Petrol	4 seats	7	1	
Peugeot . . .	Petrol	3 seats	7	2	3½-h.p. Daimler
Vacheron . . .	Gasoline	2 seats	7	3	Vacheron
Peugeot . . .	Gasoline	2 seats	7	5	3½-h.p. Daimler
Panhard-Levassor .	Petrol	4 seats	7	10	3½-h.p. Daimler
Roger . . .	Petrol	4 seats	8	9	Benz
Le Blant . . .	Steam	8 seats	8	50	Serpollet Boiler
Scotte . . .	Steam				Scotte Boiler

From the earliest infancy of the motor car until well into the twentieth century, the record-breaker's fame was as transient as it was dazzling. A record was no sooner set up than down it went again before the attack of one or other of the great names now inscribed for ever in the annals of motoring sport. The French, quick and clever (as they are in everything to do with mechanics), were not slow in seizing the opportunities presented to them by the freedom of the French roads accorded to them by their Government. Year after year they were to be found heading the winning lists with almost monotonous regularity. The Continental firms obtained a long start in the motor industry race, and it is significant that when the Paris-Rouen trial took place, Panhard-Levassor had already made 350 engines to Daimler's patent and ninety-one complete motor cars, while Peugeot had been supplied with eighty similar engines by Panhard-Levassor. Such overwhelming experience is the simple explanation of the survival of the general lay-out of the original Panhard-Levassor motor car—even down to the present day.

a superhuman endurance record of 48 hours 47 minutes single-handed driving—a feat which has never been surpassed in the history of motoring. Unhappily, he was not to live to see the development of the motor industry of the world; in the Paris-Marseilles-Paris Race of 1896, while driving between Avignon and Orange, he hit a large dog and his car overturned, and though he finished the 1,080-mile course at an average speed of about 15 m.p.h., he died mysteriously in the following year—no doubt due to internal injuries he had received in the accident.

While all these trials and racing events were being held freely on the roads of France (and for some years before) a young London engineer named Edward Butler, realising that the same motive power used by Benz and Daimler could be used for propelling cycles, took out a patent in 1884 for "the mechanical propulsion of cycles". For five years he devoted his time and money to perfecting the project. He showed a motor cycle driven by a petrol engine at the Inventions Exhibition in London during the following year and although this machine, which was the first of its kind to be made in Great Britain, actually ran in 1888, it could not be commercialised because at the time the English were denied the use of their own highways as proving-grounds for power-driven machines. Butler was, in fact, seven years ahead of his time in England, for it was not until the removal of the ridiculous restrictions by the famous "Red Flag" Act of 1896 that the roads of the country were opened to motor traffic generally.

Butler's machine, which was tested out in the early hours of the morning on out-of-the-way country roads in north Kent, was a tricycle with 32-in. front wheels by which it was steered and a single 30-in. rear driving-wheel which had its cranked axle directly driven by two 2¼-in. by 8-in. stroke horizontal water-cooled cylinders which developed ⅝ h.p. at 80 revolutions per minute and a road speed of 8 to 12 m.p.h. at 70 to 100 revolutions per minute.

The engine itself worked on the then original Clerk two-stroke cycle, in which a mixture of air and petrol vapour was exploded in the rear end of the cylinder, the other end of which formed a pump which compressed the explosive mixture into a reservoir. On the downward stroke of the piston, the mixture was admitted at a pressure of about 30 lb. per square inch for about one-quarter of the stroke, being then exploded by a low-tension electric spark formed by an insulated wiper breaking contact with the piston inside the cylinder. Current for ignition was at first supplied by a magneto, but this was later removed and a battery and coil, very similar to those used on cars today, was substituted.

Carburetion was by means of a very primitive system which depended upon the air being drawn into the cylinders being first bubbled through a tank full of petrol, both the incoming air and the mixture chamber being appropriately heated by the engine's exhaust gases.

Map of the first motor car race of July, 1894, from Paris to Rouen

Cooling was effected by connecting the cylinder jackets to a water-tank forming the driving-wheel mudguard. The weight of the vehicle was about 4 cwt.

A later model, built by Butler in 1889, had a four-cycle engine and a six-to-one epicyclic reduction gear in the rear hub, the wheels of which were cut by the local clock-maker! But though Butler's patents were acquired by the powerful British Motor Syndicate in the early 1890s, together with those of Daimler, De Dion, and over sixty other key patents affecting the position of the fledgling British motor industry, oddly enough, the Butler design seemed to be of no importance to industry, and no further development was made with it. Eventually Butler became discouraged and this amazing pioneer British motor vehicle was virtually consigned to the scrap-heap.

Then, in 1892, James D. Roots set to work on the problem of road locomotion in preparation for what he then believed to be the inevitable repeal of the road restrictions on power-driven vehicles. After making a light tricycle propelled, like Butler's, by a two-stroke engine, he went into partnership, in 1895 with a Mr. Venables and built the first British four-wheeled internal combustion petrol-driven car.

The car weighed 13 cwt. and the vertical engine, with its 5¼-in. by 6-in. stroke single cylinder, developed about 2¾ h.p. and gave the little two-seater a top speed of about 13 m.p.h.

Roots persevered and went on to build larger motor vehicles of 4 and 6½ h.p. which were satisfactory commercial machines. It must be remembered that in an absolutely new industry, such as the motor car industry in Great Britain at that time, he had no data upon which to work. He had to calculate and consider almost everything. Even the ball-bearings had to be designed and made, for in the cycle trade (in which the motor trade had its inception) it was the common thing to purchase the various small parts separately and put them together—a policy which Roots did not follow. Of course, when a motor car was imported from France or Germany, it had only to be copied. This was a comparatively easy matter and many of the early De Dion voiturettes found their way across the Channel to Coventry with this end in view. Daimler engines were also imported into England by the Daimler Motor Syndicate, and Benz cars, the first of which came to England in 1888, were sold there to the extent of over 200 in ten years.

The First British Motor Tour

In June, 1895, a 3½-h.p. Daimler-engined Panhard-Levassor car was brought into England. It ran from Paris to Le Havre, was shipped to Southampton, and then driven by the Hon. Evelyn Ellis from Datchet to Slough, Marlow, Dorchester, Farringdon, Abingdon, Cheltenham, Tewkesbury and Malvern at an all-round speed of about 13 m.p.h. This was the first motor tour ever to be made in Great Britain.

In the autumn of the same year John H. Knight of Farnham drove a little petrol car on the roads of Surrey at a top speed of 9 m.p.h. for 150 miles until he was stopped and fined by the Surrey County Council. In November a Mr. J. A. Koosen imported a motor car built by Herr Lutzmann of Dessau, and drove it for many miles in the face of stern police disapproval. In Scotland, the first motor car to run was an English-built Daimler owned by a Mr. Elliot of Kelso.

It is interesting to note that, whilst in England Knight and many others were being prosecuted for using motor cars on the road, Sir David Salomons (the organiser of the first English motor show—at Tunbridge Wells in 1895) found Monsieur Menier, the great chocolate magnate, driving about in his own car in Paris—a state of affairs showing only too clearly the technical lead which the French had obtained because their roads were open to motor vehicles.

It is interesting, too, to note the different French motor car firms which exhibited at the first motor show in that country, the *Salon des Cycles et Automobiles*, which was opened on December 12th, 1895, at the *Palais de l'Industrie*, Paris. Panhard-Levassor showed phaetons, a wagonette, a cab, an ambulance, a char-à-banc and four- and two-seater cars; *La Société Gladiateur* showed a tricycle, a tandem and a quadricycle like a two-seater pony chaise; De Dion-Bouton showed a racing steam car and petrol voiturette and Peugeot showed racing cars and voiturettes. Monsieur Roger showed cars with horizontal-cylindered Benz engines; Monsieur Delahaye of Tours (famous in later years)

The following year, 1896, was a remarkable one in the history of motoring in Great Britain, not only because British people who read their daily papers began to realise that carriages could and would go without horses—they did in France, why not in England?—but also because it

Peugeot car of 1888

showed a petrol-driven wagonette; Monsieur Loyal showed a 4-h.p. car which was greatly admired and very original; and Lepape and Gauthier also showed their own versions of vehicles driven by the new form of power.

In America, in the autumn of 1895, the Chicago newspaper, *Times-Herald*, organised a 100-mile motor-car trial in which prizes of $5,000 were offered. Of the ninety entries received, only two were ready on the day appointed for the run. A terrific crowd of spectators were present to see the start and, although the trials were postponed, the organisers offered a $500 prize for a ninety-two-mile race between the two vehicles which were ready—a 3-h.p. Benz and a Duryea. The Benz covered the distance in 9 hours 22 minutes, but the Duryea Motor Wagon Company won the first prize of $2,000 and the Gold Medal at the actual trials, which took place on November 28th— the first motor race in the United States.

was the year in which the famous Light Locomotive Act (the "Red Flag" Act) was passed and came into operation to make motoring lawful in England.

Many people thought that all the technical problems of motors had been solved and that a "motoring millennium" had arrived, but there were others who were far from sanguine as to the future of motoring. The *Lancet* thought that motor cars—particularly the Panhard-Levassor and the Peugeot—would prove admirably suitable for medical men but the *Daily Telegraph*, on the other hand, was in doubt and thought it best to 'hedge' thus:

". . . that London society will pay its guineas and go to the theatre in a private horseless carriage is not a state of things which is yet within measurable distance."

The *Yorkshire Post* was worried about the effects of the motor car on horse-owners and farmers, urging them to write to their Member of Parliament or petition Parliament against the passing of the Light Locomotive Act; but the *Sunday Times* was more progressive, and pointed out that Parisian business houses were using motor cars—and left the obvious comparison unsaid!

London to Brighton

The Light Locomotive Act received Queen Victoria's assent on August 14th, 1896. Three months later to the day, when the Act came into force, the so-called Motor Car Club organised a demonstration to celebrate the occasion. This took the form of a run of motor cars from London to Brighton—which the yearly "London to Brighton Run" keeps fresh in our minds.

In the original race, fifty-four cars were entered, but only thirty-three actually started from Whitehall Place at 10.30 a.m. on that blustery November morning. Headed by the Panhard-Levassor of the President of the Motor Car Club—the car which won the Paris-Bordeaux race, the procession passed over Westminster Bridge to Brixton. Crowds lined the

route and several of the riders got into difficulties, with the result that eleven broke down before they even reached Brixton.

Leaving Brixton, the remaining twenty-two cars headed for Reigate, where a lunch stop had been arranged for 12.30 p.m. But the crowds and the thousands of cyclists escorting the cars made driving so difficult that only ten or twelve cars had arrived, at irregular intervals, by that time and the lunch was something of a scramble. The President, Harry J. Lawson, arrived half an hour late due to the loss of a bolt. This made him three-quarters of an hour later than the first arrival. The chaos at the White Hart was such that the two Bollée motor tandem cycles driven by Léon and Amedée Bollée (Nos. 36 and 37) did not stop, but carried straight on to Brighton, where they were the first to arrive*.

There was a dinner at the Brighton Hotel Metropole in the evening. This was attended by nearly all the prominent personalities of the motorcar world of the day; Herr Gottlieb Daimler, the Bollée brothers, Sir Joseph Ewart (Mayor of Brighton), the Marquis of Abergavenny,

LIST OF CARS ARRIVING AT BRIGHTON

No.	Make	Driver	Arrival time	Time on run
35	Bollée Motor Tandem	Léon Bollée	2.30 p.m.	3 hrs. 44 mins.
37	Bollée Motor Tandem	Amedée Bollée	2.45 p.m.	4 hrs.
48	Panhard Omnibus	—	3.46 p.m.	5 hrs. 1 min.
1	Panhard-Levassor	Harry Lawson	4.52 p.m.	6 hrs. 7 mins.
3	Panhard-Levassor	—	4.53 p.m.	6 hrs. 8 mins.
22	Britannic Bath-chair	—	4.57 p.m.	6 hrs. 12 mins.
5	Daimler Phaeton	Tyrrell	4.57 p.m.	6 hrs. 12 mins.
33	Pennington Tricycle	Pennington	5.2 p.m.	6. hrs 17 mins.
15	Bersey Electric Landau	Bersey	5.4 p.m.	6 hrs. 19 mins.
8	Panhard Wagonette	—	5.7 p.m.	6 hrs. 22 mins.
24	Arnold Phaeton	—	5.14 p.m.	—
12	Daimler Dog-cart	—	5.27 p.m.	—
17	Bersey Handsome	—	5.41 p.m.	—
25	Duryea Two-seater	—	2.15 p.m.	—

* One of the two-seater Duryeas (No. 25) driven by Mr. Harrington-Moore, one of the founders of the Royal Automobile Club, as observer, is credited with having reached Brighton twenty minutes ahead of the official winner. (The Duryea was the first car to enter Reigate.)

and many other famous people were present. The drivers spent the following day (Sunday) quietly. The parade of cars fixed for that day had to be postponed owing to bad weather, but on the Monday there was an informal parade before huge crowds, in spite of the fact that a proposed exhibition of the cars on the West Pier was also abandoned as being impractical. The Daimler parcel van belonging to Peter Robinson Ltd. (No. 10), and the Arnold van advertising Sunlight Soap (No. 13), which had also completed the trip, ran up and down the Brighton front, much to the amusement of the crowds.

Several cars raced back to London on the Tuesday, the race being virtually between the Panhard which won the Paris-Marseilles Race, a Panhard Phaeton, and the Daimler Barouche *Present Times* which took part in the Lord Mayor's Procession. They arrived in London in the following order:

		Journey time	
		hrs.	*mins.*
1.	The Paris-Marseilles Panhard	3	15
2.	The Panhard Phaeton ..	3	20
3.	The Daimler Barouche ..	3	50

So ended the famous first drive to Brighton, which will always be historically remembered as celebrating the first day on which motor cars could be legally driven in England without having a man walking in front of them carrying a red flag!

1914 Brenner

Nicholas Cugnot's steam wagon of 1770

Goldsworthy Gurney's steam coach of 1827

Count de Dion on his steam tricycle of 1887

Count de Dion's petrol tricycle of 1899

Rotts and Venables' car of 1895

Panhard-Levassor car of 1894
Carl Benz's three-wheeled car of 1888

6 h.p. Daimler of 1900

*Early Serpollet steam
tricycle*

8 h.p. Peugeot motor car of 1900,
with " Handlebar " steering

CHAPTER II

A Car for the Prince of Wales

IN SPITE of the passing of the Emancipation Act in 1896, it was a considerable time before the actual manufacture of motor cars in Great Britain was under way; the earliest cars on British roads were, therefore, imported from the Continent by enthusiastic and genuinely interested persons, such as the Hon. C. S. Rolls, later of Rolls-Royce fame, who brought over a 3¾-h.p. Peugeot for his own use.

In those days, too, no self-respecting motorist dreamed of starting out on even a fairly short trip without taking a supply of food and "liquid refreshment", for breakdowns were frequent. Nuts and bolts worked loose with monotonous regularity; chains stretched; the vibrating contacts of trembler-coils had to be constantly adjusted; tyres burst and brake linings were made of camel-hair, which burned through. Worst of all, the car would often run away backwards down a hill, despite the iron sprag which was let down to dig into the road to avoid this. There were times, too, when the only way to climb a steep hill was to go up it backwards, primarily because the reverse gear was of a lower ratio than the first forward speed, but also for the reason that the petrol would run more easily from tank to carburettor when the rear wheels were higher than the front ones.

There were no windscreens, so drivers wore a kind of yachting cap with large goggles to keep out the swirling dust which rose in clouds from the untarred road surfaces of the day and turned the roadside hedgerows white in summer. The ladies wore veils around their heads to protect themselves from the dust and wind, and it was a common experience to be forced to leave one's car out in the open because hotel proprietors would not allow cars into coach-houses—they thought that the new form of transport would take away their livelihood! Even at such clubs as the famous Ranelagh, motor-car owners were frankly told that their presence was not appreciated!

Such was the state of affairs in England when motoring was young. In France, meanwhile, motoring was progressing with an irresistible rush following the 1,073-mile Paris-Marseilles race of the previous year. This had been won at an average speed of 15½ m.p.h. by Monsieur Maynard in the first car to be fitted with a four-cylinder engine—a Panhard-Levassor. The race aroused French enthusiasm, and other French engineering firms, such as Delahaye of Tours, Monsieur Darracq, and Monsieur Emile Mors, began to enter the constructional field with new systems of engine control and transmission.

Racing in France

The first French event of the year 1897 was the Marseilles-Nice-Turbie Race jointly organised by the Fêtes Committee of Nice and the Automobile Club of France (founded two years previously). Run in January over a hilly and twisting course of 145 miles, the race tested and proved the speed and hill-climbing abilities of the motor car in no uncertain manner. The 3-ton De Dion steam car, which won the race by covering the distance in 7¾ hours, covered the five kilometres (3·1 miles) between Ollioules and Toulon in under five minutes at a speed of 36 m.p.h.; whilst Monsieur Michelin, of tyre fame, averaged 31 m.p.h. between Cannes and Nice in his steam

able journey of Henry Sturmey (the founder of the British motoring journal, *The Autocar*) in November, 1895. He toured from Land's End to John o' Groats in one of the first British-made Daimler cars, and proved to many thousands of sceptical Englishmen that the motor car was a trustworthy vehicle. With admirable foresight, he had cards printed giving the information to en-

Motoring in 1900—a side-slip

car, though he lost the race through an overheated axle and the bursting of one of his pneumatic tyres—he had not had time to perfect the design!

It was on one of the deadly down-grades that the famous racing driver, Charron, and his mechanic were thrown out of their Panhard whilst passing the winning De Dion steamer. Their car turned a complete somersault and landed again on its wheels. The intrepid pair sustained no serious injuries. Nor did they stop the engine, while the steering system was repaired with a bit of wood!

No record of veteran cars would be complete without reference to the memor-

quirers that the engine was of 4-h.p.; that 10 or 11 m.p.h. was its average speed; that it could be stopped in 10 feet when travelling at its full speed; and that it cost less than ¾*d.* per mile to run.

Over in France at the same time, the proprietors of the Parisian newspapers, *Le Figaro* and *Les Sports*, inaugurated a 106-mile motor car race from Paris (Saint Germain) to Dieppe. This was held on July 24, 1897. The victor was one of seven competing Bollées, which accomplished the course in 4 hours 13 minutes at an average speed of 25 m.p.h. It is interesting to note the average speeds prevailing in the race. A four-seater

6-h.p. De Dion-Bouton steam car made 24½ m.p.h.; a 6-h.p. two-seater Panhard-Levassor, 23 m.p.h.; a 1½-h.p. De Dion tricycle, 22 m.p.h.; and a Delahaye six-seater wagonette, nearly 18 m.p.h. Monsieur Amédée Bollée drove one of his own cars; René de Knyff a Panhard-Levassor; Monsieur Lemaître a Peugeot; and Emile Mors a car of his own design. All these cars won prizes, as did each of the seven Panhard-Levassors competing.

Apart from the overturning of one of the Bollées due to careless steering, the run was uneventful. However, a most remarkable feat was achieved by Monsieur Stanislaw Grodski, who drove his Peugeot from Warsaw in Poland at an average distance of 110 miles a day for ten days, in order to take part in the race. Unfortunately, he arrived a few hours too late for the start.

But even after the Turbie, the Dieppe, and the Paris-Trouville races of 1897, the raging question of steam *versus* petrol as a power source was far from settled. In fact, many of the best brains in motoring in France were still convinced that steam would be the motive power for the road motor vehicles of the future, but the extraordinary "petrol" performances which followed soon led designers to adopt the petrol engine in preference to the steam engine, which had given and was still giving such fine results on the railways of the world.

The Marseilles-Nice-Turbie race was the only one ever won by a steam car. Continual progress in the design and construction of petrol cars soon made it possible for them to develop power superior to steam apparatus of similar weight. Though it did not have the marvellous elasticity of steam motors, the petrol engine had a peculiar steadiness and wonderful power of endurance, as had been proved in the Paris-Marseilles-Paris

race of 1895, when there was a veritable cyclone during the second and third days of the race and in the middle of one night the barometer fell over an inch.

The steam engine, too, was more vulnerable to injury, its boiler, tubing and pumps being subjected simultaneously to high pressures and violent jolts on the unbelievably rough roads of the day. Frequent stops for water were also necessary, particularly when racing against time. But in spite of all these and other disadvantages, steam cars of various makes and designs continued to be produced, both on the Continent and in Britain, for the next ten years or more.

The White steam car of the early 1900s

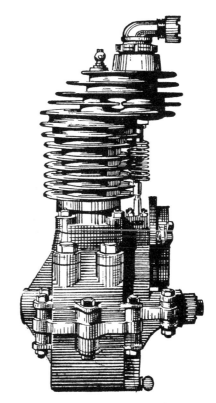

Gaillardet air-cooled engine of 1908

had a two-cylinder compound engine working at high and low pressure, of which the crank-shaft, eccentrics, guides, and other working parts were enclosed in an aluminium chamber and flooded with oil. The Turner-Miesse car boasted a three-cylinder, single-acting engine somewhat similar to Serpollet's earlier design, whilst the latter designer's car of 1906 differed in that it had mushroom valves instead of ordinary slide-valves. In all other ways, these early steam cars worked on transmission principles very similar to

h.p. two-seater weighing over 1 ton which climbed Petersham Hill at 8¾ m.p.h. under the skilful control of the Hon. H. C. Rolls. This was not a bad performance considering that few of the other competitors could do better than about. 5 m.p.h.

Hill-climbing

This hill-climbing test formed the first part of the Richmond Trials. The noise made by the cars in ascending the hill was described as appalling, and most of them

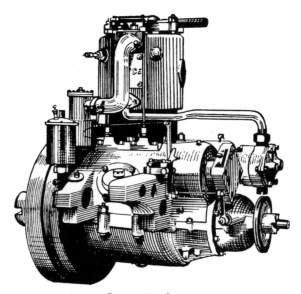

Royce engine of 1904

those used in the petrol motors which ultimately replaced them, and they looked very similar, too.

By 1899, when the Automobile Club of Great Britain held its first important motor-car trials (in connection with the Richmond Motor Show of that year), many new makes of cars were present, and some of the older, better-known producers were making cars of greater power. Panhard-Levassor showed an 8-

were enveloped in a cloud of steam. A new arrival in the world of English cars—the Lanchester—which was a 16-cwt., 8-h.p. two-seater, climbed the hill of 1 in 13 at 5¾ m.p.h.; an 8-h.p. Delahaye four-seater weighing 1¼ tons made 8 m.p.h.; and an overloaded Cannstatt-Daimler (German-built) wagonette managed a speed of from 4 to 6 m.p.h. A Benz "Ideal" two-seater with a 3-h.p. engine is reported as having "torn up" at 9¾ m.p.h.

A braking trial was also held in which the best record was made by the Delahaye, which stopped in 37 ft., when going at 16 m.p.h. down the 1 in 13 gradient. Then followed a 50-mile non-stop run from Southall to Stokenchurch and back, including the ascent and descent of Dashwood Hill. In this race the 8-h.p. Delahaye did the run in 3 hours 23 minutes, putting up the best average speed of 14¾ m.p.h., using 1½ gallons of petrol and 1 gallon of water.

Other new car makes which appeared at Richmond were Ducroiset, Hercules, Hurtu, International, Lynx, Marshall, M.M.C. (Motor Manufacturing Company), Orient (Bergmann), Phoenix, Riker, Liègeoise, and Vallée.

The same year the Club held two big tours, one at Easter and one at Whitsun. Both of these were pure and simple tests of efficiency, not displays of physical endurance and speed. The Easter tour included a two-cylinder Benz driven by Frank Butler; a Panhard-Levassor driven by S. F. Edge; a 6-h.p. M.M.C.-built Daimler driven by a Mr. Cordingley; as well as other Benzs, Daimlers and a Peugeot.

As a result of these trials and the Paris-Boulogne race of 1899, in which the Hon. C. S. Rolls represented England as a competitor, the *Daily Mail* began its weekly motoring column in September, and started publishing the results of the 100-mile English trials. The first car to run over the 100-mile course was S. F. Edge's Panhard, which was fitted with the first Napier engine ever put on the road.

Undoubtedly one of the finest trials of motor cars held in those early days was the memorable *Tour de France* race of July 16th, 1899. It was organised by the Parisian newspaper, *Le Matin*, and, bearing in mind that a one-day race can be somewhat unfair because the best car may lose because it is "off form", the race was planned to extend over seven days. The itinerary was as follows: Paris (Champigny) to Nancy, July 16th; Nancy to Amberieu, July 17th; Aix to Vichy, July 19th; Perigueux, July 21st; Nantes, July 22nd; Coburg, July 23rd; Saint Germain (Paris), July 24th.

The start from Champigny on the first leg of the 1,440-mile run was made by a 16-h.p. Panhard-Levassor driven by René de Knyff; five 12-h.p. Panhards; three belt-driven Bollées—long, powerful-looking cars; two 12-h.p. Mors; three 4-h.p. Decauvilles; eight 2¼-h.p. De Dion-Bouton motor cycles; and an Aster. Half an hour was allowed at the end of each day for repairs and a further half an hour before starting in the morning. De Knyff, the racing giant, averaged nearly 34 m.p.h. on the first day, covering 62·2 miles (100 kilometres) in 93 minutes. On the second day Charron and Girardot were running him close, with Jamin in one of

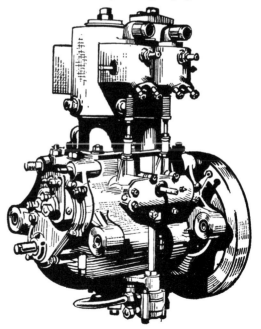

De Dion 2-cylinder engine of 1906

the huge Bollées. By the end of the day Charron was in first place. On the third day Giraud in another Bollée managed a speed of 45½ m.p.h., but with Charron still in the lead; and on the fourth day De Knyff, Girardot and Charron were the first three to finish at Perigueux.

The next day the Count of Chasseloup-Continental motor-racing news when he came in second in his 8-h.p. Panhard in the Paris-Ostend race of the following month. He also won the tourist class in the Paris-Boulogne race later in the year, yet a comparison of the state of affairs in Great Britain and in France only goes to show how very far behind the British were

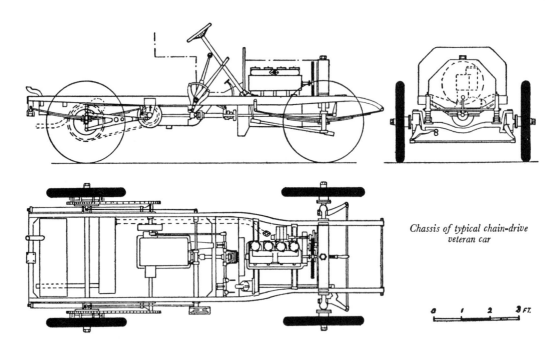

Chassis of typical chain-drive veteran car

Laubat in a 12-h.p. Panhard was first, with De Knyff second. On the sixth day Girardot was in difficulties and Charron had to abandon, whilst De Knyff, with Levegh in a Mors pressing him very hard, was still going well to win the race on the last day after having covered 120 successive miles at 37½ m.p.h. Girardot was second; Chasseloup-Laubat, third; and Pinson, in a Panhard, fourth. De Knyff's time for the whole race was 44¾ hours—an average speed of 32 m.p.h. over unbelievably rough and pot-holed roads.

The Hon. C. S. Rolls came into the in 1899 in the struggle for supremacy in the motor-car industry.

The Gordon Bennett Cup

It was for this reason that at the end of 1899 the R.A.C. decided to hold a test of sufficient interest and magnitude to attract French cars and thus prove clearly to English manufacturers just how far behind they were in design. The British public, too, which had so far been satisfied with reading in their newspapers about the exciting motor racing on the Continent, would have the opportunity to see for themselves that trustworthy motor vehicles really did exist—even though they were made abroad. Incidentally, it was in July, 1899, that James Gordon Bennett first offered the famous Gordon Bennett Cup to the Automobile Club of France.

And so, as the nineteenth century closed, the voiturette—or little car—was progressing; De Dion, Krebs, Mors, Decauville and several other French car-builders had each produced voiturettes; and Monsieur Darracq, who was then building a belt-driven Bollée, was laying down plant in Paris for turning out 500 voiturettes a year. Alcohol, instead of petroleum, was being talked about as a fuel; pneumatic tyres were the order of the day. Nice was becoming quite fashionable as an "automobile resort" for those interested in the newly-discovered sport of motor-car-racing on the speed-limit-free roads of France and Germany.

The memorable 1896 first run to Brighton was a comparatively short one, only witnessed by Londoners and Brightonians and those living along its route. The 100-mile trials of the R.A.C. had done more to foster the interest of the British man-in-the-street in motor vehicles generally. But it was the 1,000-mile Automobile Club Trial from April 23rd to May 12th, 1900, which was designed to really present the motor car to the British public. Every endeavour was made before the run to interest the authorities along the route; the police were consulted; the editors of local newspapers were informed of the progress of the organisation of the trial; and even the various road surveyors were contacted to find out the condition of the roads along the route.

The itinerary of this, the first really long motor "race" in Great Britain, is interesting, showing as it does, in many cases, the very day upon which the inhabitants of various towns had their first sight of a motor car.

April	23rd	London to Bristol (118 miles)
	24th	Exhibition at Bristol
	25th	Bristol to Birmingham, via Cheltenham (92½ miles)
	26th	Exhibition at Birmingham
	27th	Birmingham to Manchester (110 miles)
	28th	Exhibition at Manchester
	30th	Manchester to Kendal (73¾ miles)
May	1st	Kendal to Carlisle (61½ miles)
	2nd	Carlisle to Edinburgh, via Berkhill (100 miles)
	3rd	Exhibition at Edinburgh
	4th	Edinburgh to Newcastle-on-Tyne (121½ miles)
	5th	Exhibition at Newcastle-on-Tyne
	7th	Newcastle-on-Tyne to Leeds (103 miles)

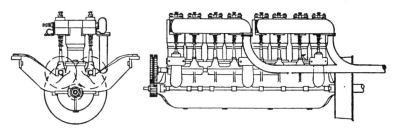

C.G.V. 8-cylinder engine

8th   Exhibition at Leeds

9th   Leeds to Sheffield (74 miles)

10th Exhibition at Sheffield

11th Sheffield to Nottingham ($82\frac{1}{4}$ miles). Speed Trials at Welbeck)

12th Nottingham to London ($123\frac{1}{2}$ miles)

This eighteen-day run of 1,000 miles was a complete success. Contrary to the general expectations, the public, instead of being unfriendly, were very enthusiastic, urging the drivers to race, in spite of the speed limit of 12 m.p.h. imposed by the police! The result was that before 500 miles had been completed intense rivalry had arisen and the general order of the day was "Step on it", as we should say today.

The Napier-engined Panhard already referred to, driven by the sportsman, S. F. Edge, fought a determined battle for days with the Hon. C. S. Rolls's 12-h.p. Panhard-Levassor, which Edge tailed so closely that time after time when Rolls was in trouble he no sooner stopped than the Napier loomed up in the distance.

But Rolls, with his 12 h.p. to the Napier's 8-h.p., had the faster car, the Panhard having four cylinders and the Napier only two. Rolls's mean speed up and down Welbeck Hill—$37\frac{3}{4}$ m.p.h. as against Edge's $29\frac{3}{4}$ m.p.h.—was evidence of this.

Eighty-three cars were entered for the trial, of which sixty-five started and seventeen failed to complete the whole run. Rolls, with his Panhard-Levassor, gained the Gold Medal of the Automobile Club of France, and Edge, in the Napier, won the Silver Medal. A 3-h.p. Wolseley two-seater and a 2-h.p. New Orleans two-seater each gained the Club's Bronze Medal. The names of many private owners who successfully drove their cars throughout the trial are now famous in the motoring world, the Hon. C. S. Rolls, J. D. Siddeley, E. M. Iliffe, and J. Scott Montagu (later Lord Montagu of Beaulieu), being among them.

The year 1900 was indeed a memorable year in the annals of British motoring. Apart from the impact of the 1,000-mile Trial on the success of the British motor industry, it was the year in which Count Zborowski created further interest by

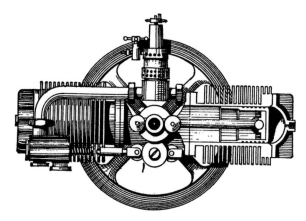

Henriod 2-cylinder horizontal engine of 1903

28

purchasing a 24-h.p. German-built Cann-statt-Daimler which, although an immense vehicle, had a very quiet engine according to the standards of the day. The year 1900 also saw the first motor gymkhana held by the R.A.C. at Ranelagh, where the aversion of the powers-that-be had mysteriously disappeared, and the anniversary of the "Red Flag" Act was celebrated by a run from London to

Girardot; they were all driving Panhard-Levassors. Jenatzy represented Belgium and Winton represented America. Charron bent an axle when cornering, but won at an average speed of 38¾ m.p.h.; Winton arrived at Orleans 2½ hours after Girardot; then he retired, as did Jenatzy. Girardot, after smashing a wheel, managed to repair it and arrive 87 minutes after Charron. De Knyff

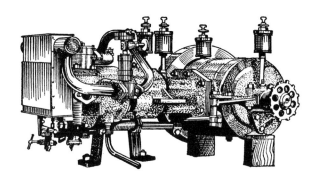

Peugeot 2-cylinder engine of 1886

Southsea, when Mark Mayhew's 16-h.p. Napier, the greyhound of the run, climbed the three miles up Hindhead in 7 minutes 16 seconds—the best time of the 103 starters, of which seventeen failed to complete the run. A trial of electric cars was also held at Chislehurst, Kent, and it was in 1900 that King Edward, as Prince of Wales, became the owner of an English-built Coventry-Daimler—an event which stimulated the motor industry to an amazing degree.

In 1900, motoring events on the Continent continued apace. The first race for the Gordon Bennett Cup was held on June 14th, from Paris to Lyon—a distance of 341 miles. France was represented by the star drivers De Knyff, Charron and

abandoned the race after breaking a gear-wheel.

Another outstanding race of 1900 was that from Paris to Toulouse and back—a three-day event run in connection with the Paris Exhibition of that year. On the first day the distance to be covered was 448⅓ miles; on the second, 218 miles; and on the third, 230 miles—a total of nearly 1,000 miles.

It was an unfortunate race in that it was run in a heat-wave, which played havoc with the imperfectly-built pneumatic tyres of the day. These gave the drivers a great deal of trouble and often placed them in exceedingly dangerous positions by suddenly bursting and rolling along the road beside the car! None the less, Levegh in his 24-h.p. Mors, which weighed over 1¼ tons, managed to cover the distance at an average speed of 33½ m.p.h. (40 m.p.h., excluding control stops). Pinson and Voigt, both driving Panhards, came in second and third respectively. In the voiturette class, a 4-h.p. Renault won with an average speed of 22 m.p.h. S. F. Edge, in a 16-h.p. Napier, had trouble with his magneto and had to retire. Antony, in a Mors, pushed his speed up to 48½ m.p.h. over a short stage of 18 kilometres.

The motoring world will always remember 1900 rather sadly as the year in which the "Father of the Motor Car," Gottlieb Daimler, died. He, like Levassor, never lived to see the development of the motor car into the approximate form which persists to this day—the form which it was to take by the end of the second decade of the twentieth century.

1914 Lorraine-Dietrich

CHAPTER III

The Hazards of the Early Motor Races

IN ENGLAND the increased use of motor cars brought with it more legal opposition. The local government boards and chief constables of many counties sought to impose regulations to prevent vehicles travelling at more than 10 m.p.h., even in the open country. They also insisted that each car should bear a registration number. It was only due to a very intense campaign by the R.A.C., in which members of the authorities concerned were given rides to show how much control the driver had over his vehicle, that the speed limit was not reduced, though the recommendation that cars should be numbered remained. However, it was not until the passing of the Act of 1903, which amended that of 1896, that cars were compelled by law to carry registration plates—or "index marks", as they were then termed.

Paris to Berlin

The principal race of 1901 was that from Paris to Berlin. It started on June 27th and ran for three days (in stages of 283, 276, and 184 miles, respectively) and it attracted the attention of the population of the Continent. The German Government gave every possible assistance in the organisation of this great event, and the warm welcome given to the French and other competitors by the German people showed how truly international the interest in the new sport had become.

The cars were classified into three groups according to their weight: (1) over 15 cwt., (2) between 8 cwt. and 15 cwt. and (3) between 5 cwt. and 8 cwt. There was also a class for motor cycles under 5 cwt. Most of the cars in the heavy group were 28-h.p. Panhard-Levassors and Mors, but there were also two immense 35-h.p. Mercedes driven by Lemaître and Werner; these, however, did not get into the first three. In the medium-weight group were four more Panhards, together with Darracqs, Gobrons, Gladiators, and a queer petrol-electric car in which the petrol engine drove a dynamo which in turn supplied electricity to drive a motor coupled to the road wheels—a Pieper. The third group, the voiturettes, was made up of 6- and 7-h.p. Renaults, one of which was driven by Louis Renault himself, and a two-seater Darracq. In the motor cycle category, 7-h.p. De Dions represented almost the whole field.

The winner of the race was Fournier. He drove one of the 28-h.p. Mors cars at an average speed of 44 m.p.h. to cover the whole distance in the net time of 16 hours 5 minutes. His car had been built under the supervision of Monsieur Brasier, who drove another of the Mors cars and who later became famous as the designer of the car bearing his name which won the Gordon Bennett Race of 1904. Girardot, in one of the 28-h.p. Panhards, came in second in 17 hours 7 minutes, and De Knyff, in another big Panhard, arrived four minutes later to take third place. Unfortunately, the British competitor, S. F. Edge, had to retire in his Napier,

Famous race-driver Nazzaro in the winning F.I.A.T. at the Targa Florio race of 1906

partly through spring trouble and partly because there were no suitable British-made tyres available; whilst the Hon. C. S. Rolls, who was driving a Mors, finished eighteenth.

It was indeed a sad day for the British entrants, for the prize-money was very attractive. Fournier's victories in the Paris-Bordeaux (1901) and Paris-Berlin races brought him well over 125,000 francs in all, for he sold the Mors, which was presented to him after winning the race, for nearly £2,000.

Incidentally, this very car had an interesting history. It was later sold to Montague Grahame-White—doyen of the motor car and, later, the flying world—for £500. He immediately fitted a rear seat in place of the racing tail and drove it to Dieppe. This was his first experience of sitting behind real power under a bonnet and of driving at speed on a public road. He was so excited that he crashed through some level-crossing gates near Paris in a fog-patch, smashed the acetylene head-lamps, and had to carry on to Dieppe with the aid of a flickering oil-lamp.

Later the Mors was fitted with a new body (subsequently known as the "clover-leaf" body) and wings of Grahame-White's own design. The old Mors radiator, which, like those of the Renaults of the time, was at the rear of the engine and was fitted at the Wolseley Works at Birmingham. The car was then driven to London. But this is not the end of the story. Grahame-White lent the car to a friend, who seemed interested in purchasing it for £1,000, and on a trial run to Portsmouth things started happening.

The Mors was easily capable of averaging 55 m.p.h. and required no small proficiency in handling. The clutch-spring was strong and the clutch very fierce, so the prospective purchaser drove all the way to Cobham in second gear— afraid to try to get into top gear! The new radiator, efficient though it was, soon boiled and water-joints started leaking. The driver left the car by the road-side and walked into Cobham! The rubber tubing was renewed and attempts were made to re-start the engine. Then disaster overtook the car. Excessive flood-

Brotherhood-Crocker car of 1906

ing of the pint-sized carburettor resulted in a terrific backfire which set the car on fire; its driver could do no more than stand at a respectful distance and watch its total destruction. So ended the

that the journey took a whole day and a night. Then when the car (and its sister car, which had travelled with it) arrived at the weighing-in, a certificate was refused for Edge's Napier because the

100 m.p.h. Napier racing car of 1905

mighty winner of the 1901 Paris-Berlin Race.

The next year (1902), at the Gordon Bennett Race, the fortunes of Great Britain turned at last, the cup being won for the first—and only—time by S. F. Edge in his 30-h.p. Napier. Mr. Austin (later Lord Austin) of the Wolseley Company had also built one 45-h.p. car and two of 40-h.p. for the race, so England was to have been fairly well represented. But the Wolseleys were not ready in time to be properly tested on the road before they were shipped to France, with the result that defects became apparent on the run from Boulogne to Paris, the starting-point of the race.

Wolseleys in France

Claude Johnson, the first Secretary of the Royal Automobile Club (the successor of the Automobile Club of Great Britain and Ireland), who accompanied Graham-White in one of the 40-h.p. Wolseleys, recounts his personal experiences in his book, *The Early History of Motoring*. They had so many adjustments to make *en route*

reverse gear did not work. The British team seemed dogged by bad luck. But within a few minutes of the closing of the weighing-in hut, the Napier was again presented for an examination; this time a certificate was granted.

The troubles of the Wolseleys, however, were not at an end. The two 40-h.p. racers had given trouble with big ends running hot on the run from Boulogne to Paris, and after a short trial of the 45-h.p. car, Grahame-White reported to Austin the defects in the lubrication system of the engine. Austin decided that Grahame-White should drive one of the 40-h.p. cars in its place.

Then the first calamity took place. Driving after midnight from Paris to the starting-point of the race, Grahame-White's Wolseley suddenly stopped dead within half a mile of the starting-point with a broken crankshaft, which he and Austin proceeded to remove by dismantling the entire engine at the roadside, fitting a new crankshaft and reassembling —a tribute to Austin's characteristic energy and determination!

The other Wolseley, now driven by Claude Johnson with Callan as mechanic, drove up to the starting line within two minutes of the time at which the race was due to start. They had barely done 200 yards of the race when the whole of the back part of the car fell out, strewing tools, inner tubes and spares all over the road! Nothing daunted, they collected some tools, threw odds and ends over the hedge, and made a fresh start. But before the first control was reached, the big ends were running hot again, and after that they had to make a stop for cooling at each control. After plodding on for thirty miles, they abandoned the race and got back to the starting-point just in time to see Austin and Grahame-White make their start in the other Wolseley twelve hours behind the departure of the last car to get away! They left at 3.40 p.m. and reached Belfort, 233½ miles from Paris, in the early hours of the morning, taking turns at driving, and overtaking five other cars on the road.

After an hour's rest, they made a start from Belfort for Basle and Bregenz, over the section of the road which was neutralised, as far as racing was concerned, by the Swiss Government. Then the contestants had to face the 5,888-ft. snow-covered Arlberg Pass, with parts of the roadside having a 1,000-ft. drop at many bends. The Wolseley was running at its best and, before reaching the summit, it passed several cars in trouble of one kind or another. It was later learnt that Max's Darracq had gone over the edge of the road some hours previously—miraculously enough, without killing Max!

Eventually the Landeck control was reached, but to the accompaniment of a violent, crashing sound from the engine. The replacement crankshaft had snapped, and for Austin and Graham-White the race was over; they rested for three days in the Austrian Tyrol and then returned to Paris.

Meanwhile, René De Knyff, Edge, and a few others had been fighting a battle on their own. Johnson took the train to Vienna; the first person he saw at Innsbruck was De Knyff—a very dejected giant. He had the race well in hand when, twenty miles from the winning-post, the car's transmission gave up the ghost, and a few minutes later Edge passed at full throttle in the low-built Napier to win the Gordon-Bennett Cup.

So it was that the Cup at last came to Britain after a succession of misadventures which were heart-breaking enough to break the spirits of less-determined men.

The Gordon Bennett Race was run in conjunction with the Paris-Vienna Race (615½ miles). Out of 137 cars which left Paris, only eighty ever reached their goal. In the heavy-car class, H. Farman, who later distinguished himself in the air, was first in one of six 70-h.p. Panhards with an average speed of 38·7 m.p.h. In the light-car (voiturette) class, Marcel Ren-

Panhard-Levassor (1902) (Paris–Vienna race)

ault, driving a 16-h.p. car of his own design, achieved the fastest time of 15 hours 47½ minutes, in spite of a half-hour penalty at controls. Farman's time was 16 hours.

Immense racers of phenomenal horse-power were coming into the field. In the *Circuit des Ardennes* the following month, Jarrott in a 70-h.p. Panhard, and Gabriel, on a Mors of the same power, set up averages of 54½ and 53½ m.p.h., respectively; while on the Dourdan route a record speed was set up by Augières in a 70-h.p. Mors of 46 seconds for the "flying mile", or 78·21 m.p.h.

Paris to Madrid

In May the following year one of the

entered in the race. This was their first bid at serious racing; pitted against three huge 110-h.p. opposed-piston Gobron-Brillies were six 90-h.p. Mercedes, which were the favourites in the race.

At Chartres, however, Renault, again driving a car of his own design, was in the lead, with Jarrott in second place. At Châtellerault the order was: Louis Renault, Jarrott, Baras in a Darracq, and Théry, closely followed by Marcel Renault in a similar car to that driven by his brother. Then came Madame du Gast,

Richard-Brasier racing car; winner of 1905 Gordon Bennett cup

most disastrous events in the history of motor-racing took place. This was the memorable speed-trial race from Paris to Madrid, when high-powered cars, which we should even today consider more suitable for the track, were run on the public roads of France.

There were no less than 230 entries in the four weight classes and lots were drawn to decide the order of starting. Ninety-eight heavy cars, fifty-nine light cars, thirty-five voiturettes, and thirty-eight motor cycles made up the field, of which Charles Jarrott, driving a De Dietrich, drew No. 1, René De Knyff No. 2, and Louis Renault No. 3.

Jarrott got away at 3.45 a.m., in one of the ten cars which De Dietrich had

a famous woman racing driver of the day, and Jenatzy, each in a 90-h.p. Mercédès. Then came disaster.

Just before reaching Ruffec, Marcel Renault, who had started thirty-ninth, was tailing Jarrott, and continued on his heels until they were overtaking Théry, when he ran into a drain. The car swung round twice and turned over on top of him, with fatal results. Maurice Farman, who was following the pair closely, pulled up to render first aid, but his friend died soon afterwards. Then on the dangerous winding road between Libourne and Bordeaux, Lorraine Barrow in a De Dietrich swerved to avoid a dog while running at over 80 m.p.h. He ran straight into a tree, pushing one of the front dumb-irons

Peugeot motor car of 1902—as restored

96 h.p. Racing Wolseley

Coventry-built Daimler motor car of 1898

10 h.p. Daimler motor car (built by Motor Manufacturing Co.)—1899

The first Ford motor car—1896

Stanley steam car of 1899

Daimler " Kimberley " motor car of 1903

Wolseley car of 1903

Delahaye surface carburettor—1901

Cowey self-registering speedometer—
1911

Close up of early Riley Vee-twin engine

Engine of 90 h.p. Mercedes of 1903 (showing overhead valves)

Wolseley motor car works in 1905

Piccadilly Circus, London, in the 1910's

20 h.p. Four-
cylinder Weller
motor car of
1903

6-8 h.p. Single-
cylinder
" Zebra " motor
car chassis of
1912

Perry light car
of 1914

of the car 6 in. into the trunk and getting thrown 30 ft. into a ditch—but both he and his mechanic were already dead.

Fate had, unfortunately, not yet finished with those intrepid drivers. Stead, also driving a De Dietrich, collided at Montguyon with the 70-h.p. Mors driven by Salleron. His car rolled over on top of

escaping with bruises. Another level-crossing accident injured Gras in yet another De Dietrich, and Jeandre and Beconnais, driving a 70-h.p. Mors and a 40-h.p. Darracq, respectively, collided at high speed, wrecking the cars, but escaping with their lives. At Angoulême, Tourand, driving a 40-h.p. Brouhot, swerved to avoid a straying child and ran

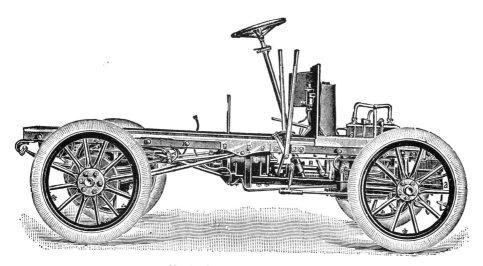

Chassis of 1904 Chenard-Walcker car

him and crushed him to death. Salleron, however, sustained no damage and drove on.

The officials at Bordeaux began to think that something serious must have happened when Louis Renault arrived first, to be followed by Jarrott and then, three-quarters of an hour later, the next arrival. Slowly the scanty but appalling information began to trickle in. Leslie Porter in a 45-h.p. Wolseley swerved at Bonneval to avoid a closed level-crossing and crashed into a house—in flames. Delaney, driving another of the ill-fated De Dietrichs, ran into a roadside heap of stones, overturning the car, but himself

headlong into the roadside crowd, killing the child, a soldier, and his own mechanic. Richard, also trying to avoid someone crossing the road, crashed into the crowd. To complete this long list of disasters, Mark Mayhew, in an English 35-h.p. Napier, crashed into a tree at Libourne as a result of the breaking of his steering-gear.

As this sad day drew to its close, harrowing stories of the dead and dying along the route began to reach Paris. Many of the drivers decided to abandon the race, and Louis Renault withdrew all his cars. Finally, the French Government refused to allow the race to continue from

Bordeaux to Spain; so serious was the view taken of the ghastly events of the day that the cars which did arrive were not even allowed to be driven to the station under their own power—they were ignominiously towed by horses.

Five English cars were entered for the race: four 45-50-h.p. Wolseleys driven by Austin, Girling, Porter, and Foster, and Mayhew's 35-h.p. Napier. None of the English cars reached Bordeaux.

Thirty-nine heavy cars, twenty-five light

it the previous year or in France. The laws of Britain did not permit such things, but after much argument a special Bill was passed by Parliament authorising the Irish authorities to close some of the public roads in Counties Kildare, Queens and Carlow to produce a figure-of-eight circuit, 103 miles in length.

To provide for public safety, and with vivid memories of the ghastly Paris-Madrid holocaust, notices were posted all along the route and in adjoining towns

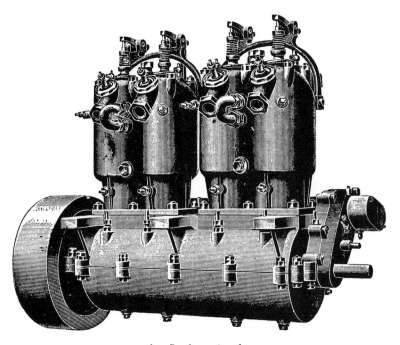

20 h.p. Brouhot engine of 1903

cars, twenty-one voiturettes, and thirteen motor cycles eventually arrived at Bordeaux, Louis Renault being the first to arrive. The intrepid Madame du Gast also succeeded in reaching Bordeaux in her De Dietrich after passing the wreckage of smashed cars along the route.

That was on May 23rd, 1903, and the next race for that year was the Gordon Bennett Cup Race, which had to be run either in the country whose team had won

warning people of the dangers of getting on the racing road. Two thousand soldiers and a large force of police helped to keep the road clear and over 270 side roads which joined the track were wired across so that stray horses and cattle were kept at a safe distance.

Racing in Ireland

Twelve cars from four countries competed: three Napiers, driven by Edge,

Jarrott and Stocks (Great Britain); two Panhards and one Mors, driven by De Knyff, Henri Farman and Gabriel, respectively (France); two Wintons and one Peerless, driven by Alexander Winton, Percy Owen and L. P. Mooers, respectively (United States); and three Mercedes, driven by Baron de Cartes, Foxhall-Keene, and Camille Jenatzy (Germany).

The race started on July 2nd, 1903, with Edge's Napier leaving at 7 a.m., to be followed at seven-minute intervals by the rest of the field. Winton, who started eleventh, was soon in trouble with a choked jet. The English competitors, too, were singularly unfortunate. Stocks mistook the road over the eastern side of the circuit and got his Napier so tangled up in the barbed wire on the side road that the car was too damaged to continue. Jarrott turned his Napier over because the steering-gear snapped, and with the Paris-Madrid race still well in mind, rumours spread like wildfire that a terrible smash-up had occurred. It was then that Baron de Cartes chivalrously stopped his car in the race at the grandstand to tell the organisers that Jarrott had not been killed, though his car was wrecked. When one considers the keen excitement of the race and the importance of every second lost, such a sportsmanlike action can well be appreciated.

Edge was now the only English driver left in the race, and he was often in difficulties, his main trouble being that of keeping the tyres on the rear wheels of the car. Then Foxhall-Keene's Mercedes broke a rear axle and soon Baron de Caters' Mercedes suffered the same fate. The American cars were eliminated one by one, and the race was won by Jenatzy in 6 hours 39 minutes, at an average speed of $49\frac{1}{4}$ m.p.h. Second and third were De Knyff and H. Farman in Panhards at average speeds of 48 and $47\frac{3}{4}$ m.p.h., respectively. Edge finished fourth in 9 hours 19 minutes at an average speed of 35 m.p.h.

It will be seen that during the nine years reviewed above the speed of racing cars multiplied itself seven times and the horse-power of engines became twenty times greater, but such impressive speeds and powers were by no means the order of the day, even on the speed-limit-free roads of France. With the end of high-speed road-racing and the building of special race tracks, the tendency was to build two distinct types of car—one for track-racing and one for ordinary use on the road. In the case of the latter the accent was gradually placed on the production of a lighter, smaller, and cheaper motor car which could easily be driven and maintained by the average man-in-the-street. At the same time larger and more powerful models were also being developed into luxurious vehicles at prices around the £1,000 mark; of these, the most famous was the precursor of the Rolls-Royce "Silver Ghost". But that is another story.

EARLY MOTOR RACING SPEEDS

	Race	Distance	Make	m.p.h.
1894	Paris-Rouen	79 miles	$3\frac{1}{2}$-h.p. Panhard-Levassor	12
1895	Paris-Bordeaux	732 miles	$3\frac{1}{2}$-h.p. Panhard-Levassor	15
1896	Paris-Marseilles	1,076 miles	4-h.p. Panhard-Levassor	$15\frac{1}{2}$
1897	Paris-Dieppe	106 miles	3-h.p Leon Bollée	23
1898	Paris-Amsterdam	943 miles	8-h.p. Panhard-Levassor	$26\frac{3}{4}$
1899	Tour de France	1,379 miles	16-h.p. Panhard-Levassor	32
1900	Sud Ouest Race	208 miles	16-h.p. Panhard-Levassor	$43\frac{1}{2}$
1901	Paris-Bordeaux	327 miles	70-h.p. Mors	$53\frac{1}{2}$
1902	Circuit des Ardennes	315 miles	70-h.p. Mors	$53\frac{3}{4}$
1903	Paris-Bordeaux	343 miles	70-h.p. Mors	$62\frac{1}{2}$
1903	Dourdan Speed Trials	Flying Mile	13-litre Gobron-Brillie	$84\frac{3}{4}$
1903	Gordon Bennett Cup	368 miles	60-h.p. Mercedes	$49\frac{1}{4}$

1914 Charron

CHAPTER IV

'Passe-partout' and Motoring Abroad

IN THE early years of the present century, while reliability trials, fuel and braking tests, hill-climbing and ordinary races were taking place in England and on the Continent, braver and more adventurous spirits were planning and starting off on motor car tours of incredible length— trips of many thousands of miles which were to test the staying power of the new form of transport to its utmost, even to destruction.

At the time of their inception, these grim, carefree world tours were looked upon, even by some of the outstanding racing drivers of the time, as utterly ridiculous, in that they could prove nothing which could not be proved by orthodox reliability trials. Looking back over the years, however, these early round-the-world motorists today claim our greatest admiration, if only because of their personal courage and resourcefulness.

In England, we must remember, motoring was still patronisingly dismissed as "the new French sporting craze", and the cartoonists of those days treated the motorist, with his goggles and fur coat, as a ridiculous figure by comparison with the carriage-owner and the horseman, whose power supply came from a unit less liable to breakdowns and accidents. When we study these pioneer long-distance drives we must bear in mind that they were made against a very frivolous background. It was only the true motoring enthusiasts who took such outstanding events seriously.

It was in 1902 that the Editor of *The Candid Friend*, a London society paper, announced his interest in the proposed attempt of a German, Dr. Lehwess, to drive a motor car round the world. Later in the year that redoubtable gentleman's canary yellow, 40-h.p., 3-ton Panhard-Levassor was duly exhibited at the Agricultural Hall, London, where it aroused much interest.

The car was a huge 10-ft.-high monstrosity, with sleeping accommodation and stores of food, spares, ammunition and fishing-tackle, and its 100-gallon petrol tank provided fuel for about a 600-mile journey. Named after Jules Verne's immortal manservant in *Around the World in Eighty Days*, *Passe-partout* cost over £3,000, and Lehwess's general idea was to run from London to Southampton, and thence to Warsaw, via Le Havre, Paris, Brussels and Berlin. Then from Warsaw his route was via St. Petersburg (Leningrad), Moscow, Nijni Novgorod, Omsk, Irkutsk and Vladivostok; across the Pacific Ocean to San Francisco, then on to New Mexico, New Orleans, Chicago, Niagara, Ontario and New York; then by boat to Liverpool and so back to London. It all seemed so simple, but everything seemed to go awry.

A start was made from Hyde Park Corner, London, in April in the presence of a large crowd, and *Passe-partout* duly lumbered off down Knightsbridge and arrived at Southampton in fine fettle. It was shipped aboard and driven off again at Le Havre, Paris being successfully reached by Lehwess and the intrepid Editor, who got side-tracked by banquets whilst the car had an overlong rest in its garage.

After two and a half months in the Gay City, however, the pair started off again for Berlin, running over a newly-devised

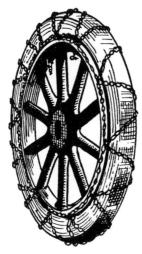

Parsons "Grippa" non-skid chain

route via Metz, Coblenz, Cologne and Dusseldorf, to reach the German capital in twelve days, after a few punctures and some ignition trouble. But it was not until September 1st, at midnight, that Lehwess started off again, to reach Warsaw ten days later; and then a week's halt was made.

Stuck in the Mud

After this the trouble started. The massive Panhard's 3 tons soon got bogged down in the soft Russian roads, and after taking to the fields as an experiment, the worthy doctor had to spend many hundreds of roubles paying the local peasants to try to haul *Passe-partout* out of the mud— without success. At Vassilykovo, the car was so badly bogged down that it took

over four hours to go 200 yards! None the less, by superhuman efforts, they averaged about forty miles each day as far as Grodno, after which the road to St. Petersburg was a little easier, the city being successfully reached and a further "rest" made.

As far as St. Petersburg, the progress of the travellers had been duly reported from time to time in the world's newspapers, but after leaving that city nothing more was heard of them until they returned by rail to St. Petersburg with the sad news that they had abandoned the car in a snowdrift near Nijni Novgorod with its cooling system frozen solid and with two cracked cylinders! The tour was at an end, but the following year *Passe-partout* was retrieved by an English second-hand car dealer and brought back to England, where its mighty yellow hulk was exhibited at a motoring exhibition in the same building where it had been shown before the start of the abortive journey— the Agricultural Hall, London!

But in spite of Dr. Lehwess's failure to girdle the world in a motor car, there were other quite sane and reasonable people who longed to motor on other roads than those in their native country, for although, on the whole, motoring was still thought of as a rich man's amusement, the motor car was hardly known outside a few highly civilised areas. It was not known in the Balkans and was absolutely forbidden throughout the provinces ruled by the Sultan of Turkey, and it was a Londoner, R. L. Jefferson, who, in 1905, decided that it was high time to drive a motor car from Coventry to Constantinople (Istambul) and thus break down the motoring barriers in Turkey.

Coventry to Constantinople

Jefferson was a well-known cyclist who had already made long Continental tours by bicycle, so the discouraging remarks of people as to the state of the roads, the bandits, and impossibility of obtaining petrol had no effect on his plans. He got a special permit from the Sultan to travel over a prescribed route from the Turkish frontier to the capital, and on September 21st set out from the *Autocar's* offices in Coventry in an 8-h.p. Rover devoid of doors and rear seats and equipped with an amazing selection of spare parts and tools. He did not intend to meet with the same fate as Dr. Lehwess.

Jefferson and an expert mechanic friend averaged 100 miles a day across Europe as far as Budapest, but beyond the capital of Hungary the roads got steadily worse and troubles began to occur. The gullies and washed-out parts of the sandy road played havoc with the car's springs, and then, when the autumn rains began, the mud became so deep that the Rover sank to its axles and had to be towed out by teams of horses.

The River Danube was followed as far as Essek, via Mohacs and Darda, and then Jefferson carried on to Semlin—further than anyone had ever travelled on that road, where, after Customs difficulties, he picked up a supply of petrol which had been sent on from Vienna by railway. But between Semlin and Belgrade—where there were already two motor cars, lay the Danube, with no means of crossing—until a barge was found on which the car was loaded and rowed across the river by four strong oarsmen.

Then, after four days in the Serbian capital, Jefferson and his friend began crawling in bottom gear over the hills to Groska, where, on a better road surface, they followed the valley of the Morava alongside the railway line at an average speed of about 18 m.p.h. But soon the road disappeared and many streams had to be forded—the bridges were in ruins—

and, after making fairly good time, the intrepid pair trundled into Alexinatz, where they were greeted by surging crowds of Serbians who couldn't speak a word of English and were no help when it came to trying to find out the state of the road ahead.

Eventually, after negotiating a wilder-

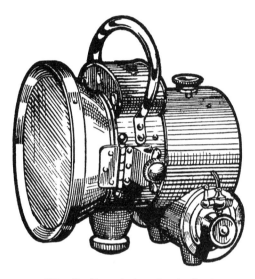

"Duco" self-contained acetylene headlamp

ness of gruelling hills and muddy valleys, Nish was sighted and the Balkan mountains loomed on ahead. But all was not straight sailing. The road was full of loose rocks which had to be rolled out of the way before any progress could be made over the mountains, though after many hours of struggling round crags and the edges of precipices, the descent was made to the valley town of Pirot, where the Mayor arranged a civic welcome and sent a telegram to the Customs officials on the Serbian-Bulgarian border ahead at Zaribrod.

Ahead lay the formidable Dragoman Pass, where the road-bridge over a river had collapsed. But with a bent front axle Jefferson managed to cross the river

51

bed, and paid a gang of mule-drivers to heave the Rover up the river bank and set it safely on the road again. And so ultimately Sofia was reached—a city which, even in 1905, was civilised and well-paved. The worst of the journey as far as natural difficulties were concerned was over, but petrol was running short: the supply promised from Vienna had got lost on the way, and it looked as though further driving was out of the question.

But Jefferson was not yet beaten. He had heard about the one motor car in Bulgaria. It belonged to Prince Ferdinand, and he visited the Prince's steward, bought a few cans of the precious liquid and pushed on towards the Turkish border through Macedonia, with its wandering guerrilla bands, who, it turned out, not only knew his name, but greeted him with great cordiality. So the run into Ichtiman, the last stop in Bulgaria, was made without incident in a sleet storm through mud and slush.

On the following day one of the front dumb-irons broke and was repaired by the roadside, and after a few more hours Phillipopolis was reached in the middle of the Fast of Ramadan. Then for two hours the drivers were held up by the sleepy Customs officials, who woke up with a start when they saw Jefferson's permit with the Sultan's signature on it. And so, after many miles of motoring along vile roads engulfed in mud, they at last bowled into Adrianople, where the whole garrison turned out to a man to watch the travellers pass through the town.

But within a dozen miles of Constantinople one of the tyres burst, and it was not until the following morning, November 5th, that Jefferson and his friend completed their 2,509-mile trip and chuffed happily into Constantinople to draw up at the Pera Palace Hotel—the first motorists to cross the Balkans. The journey had taken them thirty-one days, excluding stops.

Long-distance Tours

The year 1905 was an outstanding one for long-distance motor-car tours, for whilst Jefferson was on the road somewhere between Coventry and Constantinople, Prince Emmanuel Bibesco, his wife, his cousin and her husband, Prince George of Bibesco, Leonida—a Roumanian sportsman—Claude Anet, and three chauf-

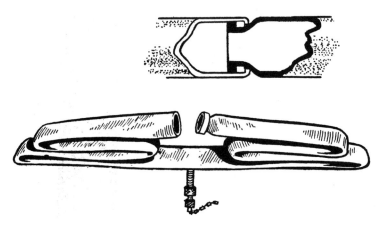

Riches detachable butt-ended inner-tube

feurs (Keller, Eugene and Giorgi) had started off in three cars from Bucharest to Teheran through unknown countries with unknown potentialities and adventures.

The team started in April in a short-chassis, 40-h.p. 1904 Mercedes, a 20-h.p.

with it the mud. The big Mercedes became bogged down and had to be jacked up and pushed clear; then the smaller Mercedes broke its springs and had to be repaired whilst the travellers picked roadside violets and cooked hard-

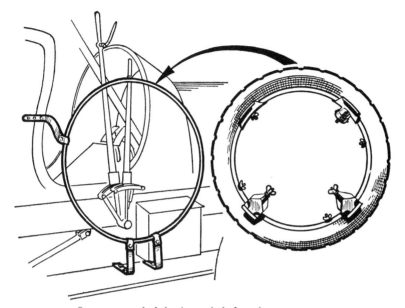

Stepney spare wheel showing method of attachment to car

Mercedes, and a 16-h.p. Fiat—all of the same year and all open tourers.

Leaving Bucharest, the party soon covered the forty miles to Giorgevo on the Danube, where a Russian ship was boarded which took them to Galatz, whence they sailed to the Russian frontier at Reni and thence to Ismail, where hundreds of people watched the cars being unloaded and started up for the run across Bessarabia to Belgrade, where a halt was made for the night.

The next day, April 13th, the 160-mile run was started to Ackermann at the mouth of the Dniester, across fields of black earth without a tree and under a grey sky at an average speed of about 12 m.p.h.! Then came the rain—and

boiled eggs and rice—washed down with vodka! But after twenty agonising hours of crazy driving, Ackermann was reached, where the Dnieper was crossed to Ovidio-pol, whence it is twenty miles to Odessa—a journey which took four hours.

On April 17th they left Odessa for Sebastopol by boat, and from there went by way of Inkerman, through Batchi-Serai and over the mountain pass to Yalta, after digging the cars out of a half-mile-long snowdrift. Then by boat to Novorossik and Batum, where a start was made on the final leg of the journey, even though the town was in the state of revolutionary siege, with bombs bursting in the streets as they left by train for Koutais and Tiflis.

Melting snows and flooding rivers ahead decided Emmanuel Bibesco to send his car back to Marseilles by boat from Batum, and Leonida declared that he would reach Teheran by motor car by way of Erivan and Tabriz, even if he had to take the thing to bits and have it carried by camels across the mountains! The rest of the party went by train to Baku and thence by boat to Lenkoran, Astara and Enzeli, and so to Teheran.

Leonida, in the big Mercedes, with five passengers and six camp-beds, eventually reached Teheran by way of Enzeli, Mendjil, and Kasvin, doing the journey from Kasvin to Teheran in just over five hours—as against the twenty-four hours taken by the rest of the party: a tribute to the car and its intrepid driver. Eventually, Keller, in the smaller Mercedes, reached Ispahan and Kum and returned to Teheran after innumerable punctures due to the heat of the Persian desert.

The motor car came of age about 1907, and its popularity in England was growing.

Steel-studded leather tyre tread—showing old "Clincher" rim

In 1904 there were only 18,340 motor cars in the whole of the United Kingdom, but by 1907 the number had grown to nearly 60,000. But in spite of this progress, which had led to the appearance of nearly 200 different makes of car, the feeling still persisted that motoring was a sport and of small practical utility. It

was largely to disprove this popular belief that a representative of Argyll Motors made a 1,353-mile tour all over England by car in ten days, noting that the same journey by available trains would have taken him about three weeks. It was also with a view of showing the practical utility of the motor car that the French newspaper *Le Matin* asked in 1907 whether any private motorist would volunteer to drive his car all the way from Pekin to Paris—a distance of over 10,000 miles. Twenty-five Frenchmen offered to do so, but only five could afford the 2,000 francs deposit demanded by the organisers.

Three French cars were in the running —two 10-h.p. De Dions and a 6-h.p. Contal motor-tricycle. There was one Dutch 15-h.p. Spyker—very similar to the one seen in the immortal film, *Genevieve*—and a 40-h.p. Italian Itala, driven by the enthusiastic Prince Borghese. The De Dions were piloted by Collignon and Cormier, the Spyker by Godard, and the Contal by Pons.

The cars were shipped to Pekin and the drivers made their own way by various routes to the Chinese capital, Prince Borghese arranging for dumps of petrol along the route. He also personally surveyed the first few hundred miles of the journey on horseback, noting particularly the width of the road in some of the mountain passes.

Pekin to Paris

It was on June 10th that the cars left Pekin in company with a large gang of coolies which the Prince had hired, together with camels and mules carrying ropes, planks, shovels and pickaxes! But immediately outside the city the road became atrocious, diving without warning into quarries and sand-pits, whilst the first river-crossing—over the Cheno—involved manhandling the vehicles up

VETERAN MOTOR-CAR HORNS

Early electric "Klaxon"

Four-note "Cavalry" horn

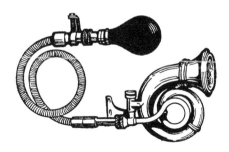

Small "Bugle" wind horn

and down 15-ft. drops at either end of the marble-slabbed roadway. Forty miles was all that they could cover on the first day before camping near Nankow.

Next day the pioneers passed through the Great Wall and managed to make Hwai-Lai, where they slept in a mud-floored inn and tried to appease their appetites with some cooked chickens which the Frenchmen had brought along; but unfortunately the birds had gone rotten in the heat! So, starting again at dawn, they crawled on to Kalgan through alternate swamps and mud, and Borghese later related how he was pushed or pulled by his coolies or their animals 150 miles from Hwai-Lai to Kalgan!

From Kalgan their route followed the dry bed of the Shisian River for fifteen miles, and then struck westward over the trackless, grassy Mongolian Plain, which was the beginning of the dreaded Gobi Desert. The going was fairly easy across the plain, a speed of 30 m.p.h. being achieved while steering by the line of telegraph poles to Pong, where the little Contal tri-car broke down and M. Pons abandoned the trip. Then came the desert, and the prospect of 800 miles of treeless territory through Kiong, Udde, and Tuerin to Urga, with bleached camel-bones glaring white in the pitiless sun.

At Urga the desert was crossed and the character of the terrain altered. The Itala stuck in a marsh and was dragged out by a team of oxen; then the Spyker got bogged down and the two De Dions hauled it out; and at the crossing of the unbridged Iro River, carburettors and magnetos had to be removed and the cars pushed across by hand. Then came the Siberian wastes, with log-cabin villages, foul inns, and bitterly cold nights, but none the less Kiakhta was safely reached, to be followed by Verkneudinsk, and the Selenga River crossed, leaving Lake Baikal

as an impassable obstacle. But Prince Borghese was not to be outdone. He led the procession over the Trans-Siberian Railway bridge, driving on the railway line. They crossed safely, but in dodging a train they fell through an old bridge over a stream and the Itala finished up on its rear end—saved by its spare tyres from damage—and had to be dragged out of the river by some Russian railwaymen.

Irkutsk, Krasnoyarsk, and Kansk were safely passed and the Kemchuk River crossed by ferry at Sellini, night-driving being resorted to to speed things up, with only oil lamps available! Omsk was reached one month and four days after the start, by way of Atchinsk and Tomsk, and a third of the journey was completed; then came Tiumen and Perm, where Europe was entered, and the fairly good road to Kazan followed.

But from Kazan to Nijni Novgorod there was no road at all! All traffic seemed to use the Volga as a means of transport. But the Itala, which was by now well ahead of the other cars, managed the journey by road, and Prince Borghese eventually arrived in Paris sixty days after leaving Pekin, having travelled from Nijni Novgorod by way of Moscow and Wirballen. The two De Dions and the Spyker arrived some three weeks later.

The following year—1908—*Le Matin*, encouraged by the success of the Pekin-Paris drive, joined the *New York Times* in sponsoring a race from New York to Paris, a "World's Cup" being offered as a trophy to the winner, who would circumnavigate the world, including the crossing of the Atlantic Ocean by ship, of course.

Six cars lined up in front of the New York newspaper's offices for the start, which was made on February 12th, President Lincoln's birthday, in the presence of some 50,000 people. There were three French cars, a Sizaire-Naudin, a De Dion, and a "Motobloc", an Italian Zust, a German 40-h.p. Protos, and an American Thomas. A Frenchman, Le Louvier, had already started on a Werner. He was not officially in the race, but he never got any further than Philadelphia.

The Thomas got as far as Hudson after hours in a snowdrift, and the Sizaire-Naudin smashed its differential less than 100 miles from New York—as did the De Dion, which was later repaired and carried on with the race.

After a fortnight of fighting with snow-drifts, the Zust, the De Dion, and the Thomas "Flyer" had only got as far as Chicago, with the Protos and the "Moto-bloc" with the veteran of the Pekin-Paris race, Godard, in charge, straggling miles behind. The Rockies were crossed, and the Thomas reached San Francisco, via Cheyenne, on March 24th, soon to be followed by the De Dion and the Zust.

After weeks of argument as to the route, it was decided to abandon the original idea to go through Alaska and across the Behring Strait and instead proceed by ship to Japan, by way of Seattle. The Thomas docked at Kobe and the Zust and the De Dion at Yokohama, and from the island crossed to Kyoto and Port Tsuruga, where a ship was taken for Vladivostok, where the De Dion was withdrawn from the race by Count De Dion.

From Vladivostok the Protos and the Thomas reached Nikolsk through knee-deep water, and thence proceeded for 500 miles along the Trans-Siberian Railway to Harbin, after which the Thomas covered 1,500 miles in eighteen days and caught up with the Protos at Lake Baikal, which the Protos crossed by rail and the Thomas by ferry-boat. Irkutsk was reached, and Tomsk, where the Protos was passed on the way to Omsk, where two teeth were torn out of the transmission of the Thomas—to be repaired after four days' work.

To cut a long, harrowing story short, the Protos and the Thomas finished the journey to Paris by way of Kasan, Moscow, Berlin and Hanover, passing and re-passing each other as each was being repaired; the Protos arriving in Paris on July 26th and the Thomas on July 30th, and after four hectic days in Paris the American car was shipped from Le Havre to New York to drive up Broadway with the mud-bespattered stars-and-stripes flag still flying proudly, as it had done for 170 days on its trip round the world. The welcome given the car and its intrepid drivers was indeed a symbolic end to the greatest motor-car race the world had ever known.

1914 Metallurgique

57

CHAPTER V

Motor Cars for the Masses

THE MOTOR CAR we know today is a direct derivative of the gas engine, for which the Frenchman Etienne Lenoir took out a patent in 1860. This engine, which used gas combined with air and ignited by electricity, Lenoir fitted into his first horseless carriage in 1862; and though he only made a few short experimental trips, his invention caused great consternation among the engineers of the day, for, unlike the steam engine, it did not burn fuel when it was not working.

Later, in 1875, a German, Siegfried Marcus, patented a similar invention and tried it out by removing the rear wheels of a cart and substituting the flywheels of his benzine motor. But it was another German, Dr. Otto, who improved and perfected the gas engine to the point at which its development was independently taken up by Carl Benz and Gottlieb Daimler.

Benz, the son of a railway engine-driver, eventually went into business as a gas engine manufacturer but, despite long hours at his factory, he spent his spare time in designing various applications of his gas engines to road traction, trying to create a motor car as distinct from a vehicle to which some form of mechanical propulsion was attached. Basically, he realised that he must have an independently-running engine, so that if the car stopped the engine would continue to run; and so that the engine could be started before the car moved.

Benz proceeded along these lines, with the two rear wheels of his first three-wheeled car as driving wheels and the front wheel as a steering or guiding wheel. The horizontal engine, with its vertical crankshaft, he placed at the rear of the car to reduce the length of the power transmission; to couple the engine to the driving wheels he took the drive forward and then brought it back to the rear wheels by a countershaft.

As the engine was placed on its side, a pair of bevel wheels were used. These drove a horizontal shaft, to which was attached a wide, flat pulley wheel. On this ran a driving belt which could be guided at will from a fixed to a loose pulley, thus freeing the revolving engine from the driving wheels when desired by moving a large hand lever which had three positions: forward, to guide the belt from the loose to the fixed pulley: centre, to run the belt on to the loose pulley; and backward, to work a band-brake on the countershaft. Such was the first attempt to produce the same effects that we get today by the use of the clutch. As to gears, Benz only allowed for one "speed" in his first car; it was only later that practical road experience forced him—he was a very obstinate man—to increase the number of "speeds".

Benz's Four-wheeled Car

This was in 1885, and the following year he included a differential in his chain-driven four-wheeled car, which allowed one rear wheel to travel faster or slower than the other when turning corners. A solid rear axle was also used, on which each wheel revolved freely, being driven by chains from a transverse shaft fitted with chain sprocket wheels and a differential drive from the engine; this method of chain-and-sprocket transmission to the rear wheels became an almost standard practice in almost every make of motor car for several years—until it was replaced, by Louis Renault, by the shaft or cardan drive we know so well today.

Benz also decided on electric ignition at a very early stage in his experiments. In his rather crude water-cooling system the single cylinder of the engine was fitted with a water jacket and a small water tank in which the circulation of the water was maintained on the "thermo" principle, i.e. the water, as it became heated, rose, and its place round the cylinder was taken by cool water. Benzine was used as a fuel instead of coal gas.

All these ideas were introduced in Benz's first motor tri-car, which had huge wire wheels and solid rubber tyres like oversized perambulator tyres. It was steered by a lever mounted on a vertical central column, and only the rear part of the car was sprung by elliptical springs attached directly to the frame of the car, which was constructed of boiler tubing. The engine boasted about two-thirds of 1 h.p., had a very large horizontally-revolving flywheel, the explosive mixture being supplied by a surface carburettor in which air sucked by the engine was bubbled through a tank full of benzine and mixed in the right proportions for the explosions by a mixing valve. Ignition was by a Ruhmkorff coil and battery.

But, as has been noticed, Benz was a curiously conservative man who was reluctant to make unnecessary changes in what seemed to be satisfactory designs. He allowed many of his ideas to become

Route of 1,000 mile trial

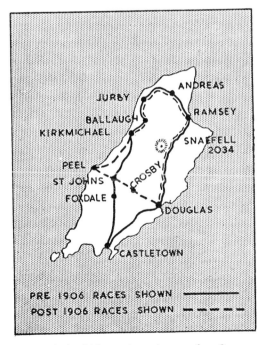

Map of Isle of Man tourist trophy races of 1906–1907

standard practice and remained obstinately indifferent to the public demand for improvements for many years. He continued to use belt transmission for several years and refused to fit a reversing gear, a gear-box, or a clutch. It was his steady refusal to incorporate these and other ideas —which were being used by other motor car designers—which led to a serious decline in the sales of Benz cars and to their complete re-design in 1903. A gear-box had, however, been fitted in 1899, and the engine placed in front two years later.

Daimler

The other co-pioneer of the motor car, Gottlieb Daimler, was the son of a master baker. He was at one time employed at Sir Joseph Whitworth's Coventry. works, but later returned to his native Germany and spent ten years working in an oil-engine works, where he became enthusiastic about ways and means of making an internal combustion engine propel a road vehicle. Wilhelm Maybach, the chief engineer of the works, shared his enthusiasm, and in 1882 they both resigned and founded an experimental workshop at Cannstatt.

By 1883 Daimler had invented "hot-tube" ignition for the oil engines he produced at Cannstatt, and then he built a $\frac{1}{2}$-h.p. motor cycle with a frame constructed of wood and iron, resembling an old-fashioned hobby-horse, with the rider sitting over the amidships-mounted engine on a sort of horse saddle! His son Paul actually rode the machine for the half-mile from Cannstatt to Unterturkheim and back on November 10th, 1885, and Maybach used it occasionally. Then, after trying his engines out on boats and sledges, the two engineers set about building the first four-wheeled, petrol-driven vehicle the world ever saw.

A horse-drawn carriage was purchased, and alterations were made to it to make it strong enough to take the vertical 1½-h.p. engine, with its air-cooled single cylinder and hot-tube ignition, which drove the rear wheels through simple spur gearing and a very crude form of differential arrangement which consisted of leather discs which slipped when one of the back wheels revolved at a different speed to the other. This famous vehicle—the first successful four-wheeled, petrol-driven motor car in the world—is now preserved in the *Deutsches Museum* at Munich.

Daimler motor tramcars, boats, fire-engines and even the first public motor taxi-cab in the world followed in rapid succession, but Daimler and Maybach were still keenly desirous of developing the motor car as cheap transport for the masses; and after building the first lighter-than-air dirigible, propelled by a 4-h.p. single-cylinder engine, in 1888 and selling motor boats by the hundred, work was commenced in 1889 on a "Vee" twin-cylinder engine—similar in its essentials to those of today—which was fitted into a car somewhat resembling Daimler's first effort.

Soon followed a two-seater, four-wheeled car with the famous and revolutionary "Vee" twin engine mounted at the rear, and almost every part of the vehicle, including the wheels and tubular frame, made of steel. The engine was cooled by a water jacket round the cylinders, the cooling water being circulated through the tubular frame of the car—a method which has been tried out during recent years on modern racing cars with the object of saving weight! Power was transmitted through an exposed train of gears to the rear wheels, the gear ratio being variable to suit the gradient.

Daimler and Maybach both went to Paris in 1889 for the World's Fair, at

Dashboard view of 1902 *Wolseley motor car*

Chassis view of 1902 *Wolseley motor car*

1. Track Rod	8. Lubricators	15. Gearbox	24. Brake Cross-shaft (Hand)
2. Front Axle	9. Steering-wheel	16. Gear-change lever	25. Brake Cross-shaft (Foot)
3. Steering-gearbox	10. Steering-column	17. Gear-lever quadrant	26. Rear Axle
4. Engine fly-wheel	11. Foot-brake	18. Hand-brake lever	27. Brake Drums
5. Engine (horizontal)	12. Clutch	20. Exhaust Pipes from Engine	28. Fuel Tank
6. Starting-handle bracket	13. Oil Tank	21. Silencer	29. Lamp Brackets
7. Dash-board	14. Engine to Gearbox Drive-chain	22. Rear Chains	

200 h.p. Vee-eight-cylinder racing car of 1908 (Lee Guiness in the driving-seat)

7½ h.p. Wolseley motor car of 1903 with detachable wheel rims

*At the top of Hand Cross Hill, Sussex
in 1906*

*90 h.p. Racing
F.I.A.T. driven
by Felice
Nazzaro —1908*

Rougier on a De Dietrich climbing Mont Ventoux Hill—1907

Humber motor car of
1902

Two-seater Riley
motor car of 1910

which their interesting two-seater car caused a great sensation when it was exhibited and demonstrated. Before returning to Germany Daimler granted full manufacturing rights to the widow of Edouard Sarazin, who had been Daimler's agent in France. As it happened, Madame Sarazin later married Emile Levassor, who was a partner with René Panhard in a Paris firm of woodworking machinery manufacturers, and on her marriage she placed the valuable Daimler patents in the hands of her second husband.

All this may seem irrelevant to the constructional principles involved in motor cars of the beginning of the present century, but, in fact, the ultimate passing of the Daimler rights into the hands of Panhard-Levassor can be said to be the very first brick in the mighty edifice of the French motor-car industry upon which the world was virtually to depend for its motor cars for several years—before the industry spread abroad on a really large scale.

Levassor

But Levassor felt that Daimler's talent lay with engine design rather than with the planning of the motor car as a vehicle, so he started designing his own type of car, placing the engine at the rear of the vehicle, amidships and finally in front, where, as we have already mentioned, the vast majority of modern cars have their engines. Indeed, the motor car of today is substantially the same in layout and functional plan as Emile Levassor's cars which took part in the Paris-Rouen trial of 1894.

Of the ridiculous and antiquated English laws governing the use of self-propelled vehicles in Great Britain, no more need be said, but it is interesting to note that from 1895 Benz cars were handled by Henry Hewetson and Walter Arnold of

Peckham, London, both of whom took part in the original "Brighton Run" of November, 1896. Daimler himself had nothing to do with the development of the motor car in England, where cars were manufactured under his patents by the English Daimler Motor Company of Coventry. Such were the beginnings of the British motor industry.

The famous Daimler "Vee" twin engine was mounted across the chassis of the car in the same position as that used today on B.S.A. and Morgan three-wheelers, and in the search for more power the logical thing to do was to increase the number of cylinders. So by 1898 a four-cylinder engine and a 6-h.p. "racing car" were produced at Daimler's works, a six-seater the previous year, and the first petrol-driven motor bus in the world started running between Mergentheim and Künzelsau, in Württemberg, in 1899.

During 1898 and 1899 a Cannstadt-built Daimler racing car of 28 h.p. crashed; the foreman of the works was killed whilst racing it, owing to it being dangerous and completely unmanageable because of its high centre of gravity and very short wheelbase. But largely due to this accident, a car which was to revolutionise motor-car design was evolved, the world-famous Mercedes, which was the brain-child of Daimler's son, Paul, and Wilhelm Maybach—a car which swept to victory in the races in the South of France, as we have already seen.

The Mercedes

To say that the Mercedes cars made a great impression on the motor industry of the world—even in those early days—is by no means an overstatement; for in a brief five years, every car, whatever its make, became sadly out-of-date. The Mercedes cars, with their pressed-steel chassis, honeycomb radiators, gate-change

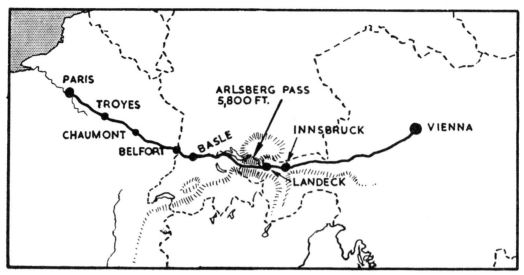

Map of Paris-Vienna (Alpine) race

gear-boxes and steeply-raked steering wheels, were years ahead of their time. Above all, the touring cars were almost completely silent when their engines were "ticking over". If modern cars are examined—cars which have just come off the production line—we can still see a number of outstanding features which were initiated by the Daimler-Maybach partnership way back in 1900, features which were immediately copied by every motor-car manufacturer in the world.

But while all this development was taking place on the Continent, there was an English engineer who had been following the progress made by others and conceiving ideas of his own. His name was F. W. Lanchester; with his brothers, Frank and George, he was not only to add his part to the subsequent development of the Lanchester car, but to the story of his country's motor industry.

In 1893 the Lanchester brothers produced a small 3-h.p. single-cylinder engine which ran at the then high speed of 800 r.p.m. This they fitted into a boat propelled by a stern paddle-wheel; and two years later, after endless planning and personal work, the brothers succeeded in producing a 5-h.p. motor car of completely unusual design. The chassis was built of 2-in. steel tubing, and the engine, with its two geared crankshafts and flywheels, was placed amidships, with its single cylinder inclined horizontally in a forward direction. The driving axles were coupled by a differential gear, and power was transmitted from the engine through a sprocket-driven epicyclic gearbox, the gear ratios being changed by a pedal; while, instead of the pedal type of accelerator, the speed of the engine was controlled by a "knee-swell" arrangement, similar to that used for volume control on American organs and harmoniums.

Everything on that car was unorthodox. There was no springing on the chassis or the mechanism except for the cushioning provided by the specially hand-made $2\frac{1}{2}$-in. Dunlop pneumatic tyres. The body, which was suspended on the chassis by three springs, consisted of steel side-plates and eight transverse steel tubes, the side plates being sheathed with polished walnut. Incidentally, the carburettor, which was fed with petrol by a hand-pump, was of the "wick" type, which depended for its operation on the capillary action of a cotton wick and the evaporation of the petrol soaked up—a system which in varied forms persisted in Lanchester cars until 1914.

As an example of the technicalities of a veteran motor car of the turn of the century, the 4-h.p. twin-cylinder model produced by J. S. Critchley of the English Daimler Motor Company may be described in some detail, for it was one of these cars which was driven by Henry Sturmey, founder of the *Autocar,* from John o' Groats to Land's End, a journey which took ninety-three and a half hours running time—an average speed of 10 m.p.h.

The engine had automatic inlet valves and tube ignition; cooling water was carried in a tank at the rear below the level of the engine, from which it was pumped by a rotary pump, friction-driven from the flywheel; the radiator consisting of lengths of copper tubing to which fins were soldered to catch the air. Transmission was by a huge revolving clutch to a massive three-speed gear-box,

and the final drive was by way of a differential gear mounted in the centre of a transverse shaft which carried chain sprockets, whence block-chains carried the power to the rear wheels, which were shod with solid tyres. Steering was by tiller, and the engine had no throttle, but ran at the invariable speed set by a centrifugal governor which cut out the exhaust valves and was controllable in its setting by what became the accelerator pedal on later cars. The speed of the car was thus controlled by changing into a higher or lower gear—a frequent and very tiresome business.

The braking system, like that on most very early motor cars, was the Critchley-Daimler's weakest feature, for the foot-brake operated on a contracting band hanging loosely on the chain-sprocket shaft, which meant that if one of the side chains snapped—a frequent occurrence—the foot-brake was useless. The hand-brake worked on a leather or wood-block lined band which contracted on drums bolted direct on the rear-wheel spokes, which were of wood, so that a long downhill coasting run might finish up in disaster,

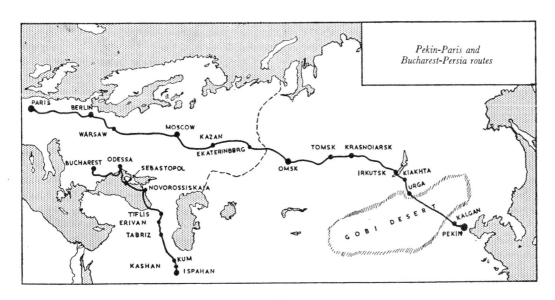

Pekin-Paris and Bucharest-Persia routes

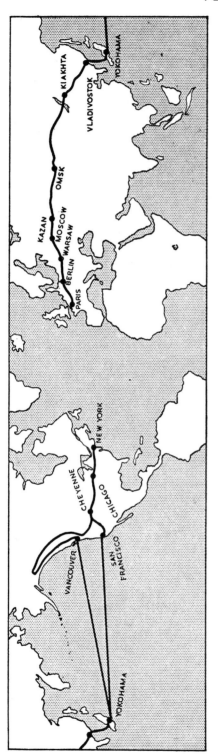

Map of New York-Paris race

owing to the brake-band linings catching fire! There was a third brake, called a "spoon brake", which pressed down directly on the tyres, and as a final "precaution" there was a steel-shod spike or "sprag" which could be let down while a hill was being climbed, which would—or should!—dig into the rough road surface and prevent the car running backwards should the engine fail! Yet withal it was on one of these cars that King Edward VII as Prince of Wales made his first trip in a motor car on a public highway—at Warwick Castle in June, 1898.

British Cars

By 1899 in England new cars and new motor companies were getting to be quite commonplace. The Humber Company, an offshoot of the Humber Cycle Company, produced a two-seater "sociable", which was powered by a 2½-h.p. Léon Bollée air-cooled horizontal engine with enclosed bearings and sight-feed bearing lubrication. The Star Motor Company, too, announced a new programme with the unheard-of speed of delivery within seven days of order! But of all the cars later to be famous there is no better example than the Riley, which had a modest beginning in a little single-cylinder 2¼-h.p. air-cooled engine which drove the rear wheels by way of a flat belt and was the first car engine in the world to be fitted with mechanically-operated inlet and exhaust valves—and that was in 1898.

Riley, like Daimler, Wolseley, Lanchester, Humber and several other makes, can boast an unbroken link with the very beginnings of the motor industry, but there were other makes in the veteran days which, for one reason or another, disappeared from the market, even though they were fine productions. Even the famous Napier firm, which in 1904 had exhibited at the Crystal Palace Motor Show a superb 6-cylinder 30-h.p. car which would run perfectly from walking-pace to 50 m.p.h. in top gear, even though chain-driven, disappeared from the market as makers of motor cars. Other firms, such as Wilson-Pilcher, who produced in the same year an 18-24-h.p. six-cylinder car with a constant-mesh gear-box, were absorbed—this particular company by Armstrong-Whitworth.

Some idea of the way in which the British motor-car market was being supplied can be gained from the fact that in 1903 Britain was the largest purchaser of motor cars from France—over £2,000,000 worth being imported during that year. None the less, at the following year's Paris Motor Show, Napiers, M.M.C., Hoziers, and Hotchkisses were being exhibited.

By 1904 "hot-tube" ignition had disappeared from engine design; beehive-type radiators and cooling fans had become general; mechanically-operated inlet valves—which Percy Riley had introduced in 1898—had become general. Pressed steel was beginning to be used in place of wood, sandwiched between thin steel plates for chassis, and singly-cast cylinders in multi-cylinder engines were much in fashion, whilst the cylinder bore was generally equal in size to the stroke—or even larger.

But there were also some queer ideas afoot in those remote days. The Hutton car of 1903, with its hydraulic infinitely-variable gear operated from the steering column, is an example; whilst to make for a more pleasant journey on the atrocious roads of the day spring-wheels, such as the "Glyda" and the "Empire", were put on the market, but their popularity was shortlived.

By 1908 chain drive had almost entirely disappeared and car construction was becoming more conventional. Simplicity of design was being studied more and more, together with ease of access to parts needing constant servicing—in contrast to our present trend! Cylinders were beginning to be cast all in one block, and in many cases—such as that of the "Motobloc"—there was a tendency to cast the engine crankcase and gear-box in one unit. Thermo-syphon cooling-water circulation was coming into favour, and the leather-faced cone clutch was in the majority, followed a close second by the multiple-disc clutch—a modification of Professor Hele-Shaw's effort of many years previous.

In 1913 came the eleventh International Motor Exhibition, which was held at Olympia, London. It was hardly an "international" show, however, but one of a closed society, in which American firms making many thousands of cars each year were not even represented—cars which had never been seen in England. But at that show there were many British and Continental motor cars to be seen—cars which had improved out of all knowledge over the previous six or seven years. They ran with far less smell and noise, and their comparative silence threw into much greater prominence the noisy gear-changing of the day, apart from which some of the best and most expensive cars could only be heard by the noise their steel-studded tyres made on the road.

Progress in Design

But even before the First World War cars had their troubles. Better gear-wheels and gear-boxes eventually quietened things down a bit, but breakdowns with badly-designed bevel gears in back axles led to the adoption of worm drive, with its lubrication problems. Similarly, added experience caused the abandonment of the previous practice of mounting very small high-speed engines in heavy cars. Large engines running at slow speeds were used instead, and it is odd that the practice should now be again reversed, with the result that at 50 m.p.h. the average present-day car engine of 7 or 8 h.p. is turning over at 5,000 or 6,000 r.p.m.—and wearing itself out in the process much more quickly

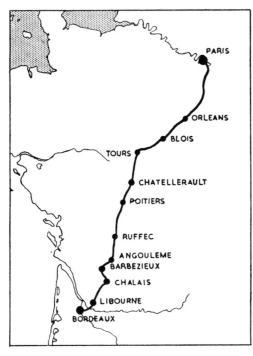

Map of Paris-Bordeaux race

than the slow-speed, more powerful engine of forty-five years ago.

In those immediate pre-war days—the golden era of veteran and Edwardian motor cars—many ideas which we accept as commonplace these days were first seen. Multi-cylinders were cast in one unit together with exhaust and inlet manifolds, multi-bearing crankshafts were becoming more common as the bending stresses of a shaft turning at high speed

were better understood; engines were beginning to look neater, and piston valves and rotary valves were tried out with more or less success, though poppet or "mushroom" valves were used in the majority of cars. Valve camshafts were usually chain-driven, high-tension magneto ignition was almost universal, thermo-syphon and engine-driven pumps were used either singly or together for engine cooling, and some gear-boxes were mounted on the rear axle.

There were also steps backward in design—backward by present-day judgment. The two-cycle engine, at one time popular, had almost completely disappeared from the market; and the front-wheel brakes fitted many years earlier by progressive designers to reduce the chances of the deadly side-slip practically disappeared again, whilst wire wheels, which had been quite fashionable back in the late 1890s, were declining in favour, though they were fitted as standard by some manufacturers.

In some things, English designers were rather backward, as in the case of the self-starter. They contented themselves with making a motor car which would run reliably and gave little thought to the starting of its engine. In the United States the 1911 Cadillac boasted an electric self-starter of similar operational design to those installed on modern cars, whilst the American compressed-air starters operated from a high-pressure air container into which air was pumped by the engine when it was running. This air supply was also used for pumping up tyres and for jacking up the car. Laurence-Scott electric self-starters were used in 1912 on Crossleys and compressed air on Adams cars, whilst some makes used electric-acetylene, in which a charge of acetylene gas was forced into the cylinders by a hand-pump and exploded by a small hand generator mounted on the dash-board.

By 1913, motor car bodies could be seen in every colour and combination of colours, whilst some of the "sporting" bodies of the day were boat-shaped, with side-sheets overlapping in the approved clincher-built boat style. Punctures due to the flinty roads of the time were more or less offset as a nuisance by the advent of detachable rims and wheels, and the famous "Stepney" spare rim, which could be clipped to the rim of a punctured tyre, did much to make the motorists' lot an easier one, though the fitting was not included in the price of the car. From about 1912, however, five wheels and tyres per car were expected by the purchaser—and not as an extra!

Probably one of the most outstanding and unique cars of the 1913 Motor Show was the Hupmobile, which boasted a centrally-placed gear lever, a pressed-steel floor, and an electric starter-motor which was engaged and disengaged with teeth cut on the engine flywheel by a pedal located to the left of the clutch pedal. The Hudson car of the day was fitted with a cork-faced clutch.

The extent to which the motor vehicle was beginning to enter into public life can be judged by the fact that in the year 1907 there were only 3,777 power-driven vehicles registered in the London Metropolitan Area as against 12,700 horse-drawn vehicles; but by 1912, these figures were almost completely reversed: 13,800 power-driven vehicles and 2,800 horse-drawn ones. It was a sign of the times. Incidently, due to the advent of more reliable tyres and high-tension magneto ignition, there were no less than 130,000 motor cycles on the roads of Great Britain in 1913.

1915 Bianchi

CHAPTER VI

Pre-1914 Trials and Tribulations

LOOKING AT a modern car, it is almost impossible to realise the crudeness of the vehicle from which it was developed, for even after the first ten or fifteen years of continual improvement the motor car of 1910 left much to be desired. It was not too reliable, it was far from comfortable, and gave its passengers but scant protection from the weather—which was then, in England particularly, as unreliable as ever.

For the driver and his partner in the front pair of seats, windscreens had arrived on the scene—but, of course, without screen-wipers; whilst for side protection from the elements celluloid side-screens were occasionally fitted; but the unfortunate passengers in the rear seats of a four-seater car had to be protected by a special rear-seat wind screen —an extra on the price of the car—which was supported by movable arms fixed to the sides of the car body. Motoring under such conditions was indeed a very draughty business, and motorists of the day must have surely been "tough" in more senses than one.

Naturally, as the saloon car had not yet appeared, it was impossible to arrange for the heating of the interior, for even in the case of the enclosed landaulette the floor-boards and collapsible half-hood were far from windproof; so that, even if the passenger was travelling in some sort of comfort, the unfortunate driver or chauffeur was usually perched well out in the elements in front of the closed carriage,

sheltered only by a vertical glass screen the angle of which could not be altered.

Tyres

Tyres, as has already been mentioned, were prone to give an enormous amount of trouble on the road—particularly in wet weather. This was due to the roads being in the main composed of steamroller-crushed flints, the tiny flakes of which easily entered the tyres, when their entry was effectively lubricated by water. To combat this evil, many ideas were put forward, for a "blow-out" on a tyre in those days was indeed a hectic experience, high-pressure tyres being used, carrying a pressure of anything from 60 to 90 lb. per square inch—depending on the size and weight of the car they had to carry. They went off like a cannon and left one's ears ringing. Such tyre pressures are about three times those in use today with low-pressure tyres—or "balloon" tyres, as they were called when they were first introduced.

Tyres being what they were, and punctures more or less inevitable, tyres were mounted with ready inflated tubes on spare rims—such as the "Stepney"— which would clip alongside a punctured tyre, and in other systems either the rims or whole wheels of the car were made readily detachable, and the portable jack made its appearance, by which the car could be lifted whilst a change-over was being made.

Mention of a jack calls to mind the

fact that the motor cars of the first decade or two of the twentieth century were supplied by the makers with a very full kit of tools at no extra cost—an idea which seems these days to have been completely forgotten. Indeed, it is on record that one at least of the modern car manufacturers contemplate still further reducing the car's tool-kit, having already decided that a starting handle is completely unnecessary and not even leaving a hole through the metal sheeting at the front of the car for its use in the event of the self-starter motor jamming. Surely this would seem to be technical advance in reverse!

Lamps

Conversely, in the very early days of motoring running lamps were never included in the overall price of the car, but constituted extras which the owner could purchase to suit his own taste and pocket. Oil side- and tail-lamps were the order of the day, with powerful acetylene gas headlamps with diameters up to 18 in. which gave a beam far more bright than some of the electric head-lamps seen on cars today. But both oil and acetylene lamps were far from reliable. A strong gale or a bumpy road would often extinguish them, and in the case of the oil tail-lamp, many was the unsuspecting motorist who was fined heavily for not having his tail-lamp alight. Some of the later designs, however, were provided with clear-glass side-windows in addition to the red glass facing to the rear, so that not only was the number-plate illuminated, but a shaft of light was thrown across the road on the off-side which the driver could see by turning his head when he wished to check on his rear-light.

Another great difficulty with the lamps of the early 1900s was the continual breakage of their glasses by stones thrown

up by the wheels of passing cars—an eventuality almost non-existent today. Flying flints were also the reason for the radiator stone-guards which have persisted to this day on some makes of sporting cars.

On pre-First World War two-seater cars, waterproof fabric hoods—called "Cape cart" hoods, after those used on South African two-seater buggies—were fitted, ash hoop-sticks hinged from points on the body carrying the fabric and the

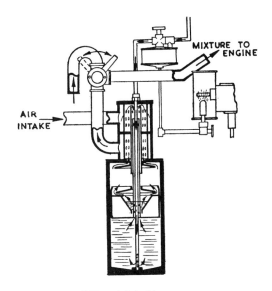

"Hot-tube" ignition system

extended hood being retained in place by straps taken down to either the dashboard or front wings. This gave protection of a kind, but a "scuttle" was soon fitted to the dashboard, on which a windscreen was fitted, which, together with side-doors, gave the driver additional protection.

Today, the lubrication of the engine and gear-box is entirely automatic—the driver does not even have to give it a thought—but back in the 1910s most cars were fitted with an oil tank and individual drip-feeds, which were mounted right in front of the driver on the wooden dashboard. These glass-encased drip-feeds had to be under constant inspection, and had to be regulated from time to time, according to the weather. On a cold day, when the oil would not flow freely, the regulating needle valves would have to be opened up, whilst on a hot day they would have to be screwed down. Engine temperature also entered into the picture, so that if he wanted a trouble-free journey it behoved the driver to keep a very careful eye on his oil-supply indicators, which checked the

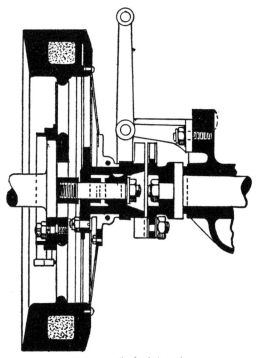

First magnetic clutch (1904)

oil distributed to front engine bearing, rear engine bearing, clutch-shaft and gear-box.

Lubrication

On some makes of car, the oil dripped by gravity from the oil tank, but in others an engine-driven pump on the oil tank pushed the oil under pressure through the regulating valves, whence it descended

to its appointed place by gravity. This last method had the added advantage that the faster the engine was running the more oil was distributed to the various points—but still in a pre-set proportion.

But the checking of the drip-feeds was not the only oil problem confronting the car-driver in those days. He had to be sure that the oil-level in the engine sump was maintained at a proper height, for on that depended the lubrication of the big-ends, cylinder walls and little-end gudgeon pins. In most cars the lubrication of these parts was achieved by "splash"—that is, the big ends, as they rotated, dipped into the oil in the engine sump and splashed it around in the crank-case, thus distributing it where it was most needed. Thus if the sump oil-level was allowed to fall, before the unfortunate driver knew what was happening the pistons had seized up solid in the cylinders or the white metal in the big-end bearings had got so hot that it would run out and cause the engine to "knock".

Today, of course, all is different. Oil is still placed in the sump and its level checked by a dip-stick, but thereafter everything is automatic. An engine-driven oil-pump, submerged in the oil-sump, sucks in the oil and forces it under a pressure of from 15 to 50 lb. per square inch to all the moving parts of the engine, starting usually at the rear main engine bearing and proceeding thence through a hole drilled through the crankshaft to each big-end and main bearing in turn. From the big-ends, pipes are fitted up the connecting rods to convey oil to the hollow gudgeon pins inside the pistons, whence the cylinder walls receive their quota. A separate pressurised supply direct from the pump is also taken to the gears driving the valve camshaft and to the camshaft itself, and all the oil thus distributed eventually falls back into the sump to start on its journey again. All the driver has to do is to watch the oil-pressure gauge on the instrument board.

A brief comparison between the motor cars of 1900 and those being produced immediately before the start of the First World War gives an opportunity to see the trend of car design in the course of a brief fourteen years. As we have already seen, the cars of 1914 were mainly four-cylinder machines with mechanically-operated inlet and exhaust valves, whereas those of 1900 had single- or two-cylinder engines with automatic inlet valves operated by the suction of the piston, whilst the high-tension magneto had almost entirely replaced the coil-and-battery system and automatic lubrication the oil tank and separate drip-feed. Improvement in design of carburettors, together with magneto ignition, had resulted in giving engines a much greater range of speed and a greater top speed, which again made the engines more flexible and less dependent on continual gear-changing.

On the other hand, gear-box, back axle and clutch had undergone but little change during the period, though some designers were incorporating the gear-box with the back axle, which meant that a motor car could be built up of five units: engine, back axle, front axle, steering-gear and chassis, radiator, and petrol tank—a combination which was at the time con-sidered to be more economical and efficient to manufacture than the engine-gear-box unit.

So the eve of the First World War saw a very different type of motor car from that of fifteen years previously—not only in the technical improvements of the vehicles themselves, but also in minor detail developments aimed at providing for the owner's convenience and personal comfort. Windscreens, as we have already seen, luggage grids—the "boot" had not been even thought of—spare-tyre-carriers, and steering wheels coated with celluloid began to make their appearance. Triplex safety glass—invented by a Frenchman—and Sankey all-steel wheels were also inventions which contributed to the success of the motor car during the fourteen years under review, the latter being fitted as standard to Arrol-Johnston, Austin, A.C., Argyll, Belsize, Clement-Talbot, Daimler, Ford, Humber, Lanchester, Morris, Rolls Royce, Rover, Sunbeam, Singer, Standard, Vauxhall and Wolseley cars of 1914—a tribute to the importance of the invention. Joseph Sankey Ltd. also produced quickly-detachable types of wheels and rims, including the Warland, Stepney, and other then popular types.

Brakes

Higher road speeds brought with them the demand for better brakes—brakes more reliable and longer-lasting—and

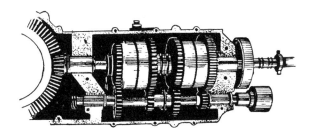

De Dion two-speed, constant mesh gearbox of 1904

to find an ideal material for brake-shoes, cast iron, hardwood, brass and impregnated compressed cotton were all tried and discarded. Then came Henry Frood's famous invention—"Ferodo", a spun material of asbestos and fine brass wire impregnated with bonding chemicals which gave his brake-linings great dura-

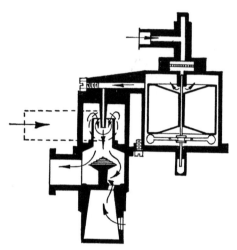

Daimler "Surface" carburettor of the 1890's.

bility and resistance to high temperatures. Frood's company was formed in 1902, after he had got the germ of his idea by noticing that the brake-shoes on farm wagons were often repaired by nailing old boots over the old worn-out brake-shoes. Hence the term we still use today —"brake-shoe".

In the days before the First World War, the body-work of the better-class motor cars—Bollée, Daimler, De Dietrich, Renault, Rolls Royce, and other famous makes—was made of hand-built wooden coachwork, not of pressed steel, as is the case today. Some of the earliest firms of coach-builders making bodies for the first motor cars built in Great Britain had been in the business for hundreds of years making bodies for horse-drawn stage and

mail coaches and private carriages and landaus. They were past-masters at their trade, and each car body made was a "one-off" job, usually built to the car-owners' individual taste, for in those far-off days, when one bought a motor car, one bought the bare chassis: the body was an "extra" which one purchased separately and had fitted. Today the reverse is the case, for one selects one's car more by its body-work and internal fittings than by the engine and the mechanical functioning of its power unit.

Admittedly, the Edwardian veteran touring car at its best had an easy and refined performance, with its high-powered engine, heavy flywheel and high gear ratios. It had the sensible springing which was a relic of earlier days and comfortable coachwork—some makes being fitted with luxurious limousine or limousine-landaulette bodies; but such expensive motor cars were in no sense cars for the man in the street—they cost too much to run. He needed something light, reasonably inexpensive, easy to handle, and capable of being locked round sharp corners and garaged in a small shed; and it was to meet this ever-increasing demand that the 10- to 15-h.p. light two-seater car was introduced, which was, in effect, the old racing phaeton or "spider"—the two-seater voiturette fitted with a four-cylinder engine.

So in the days immediately before the outbreak of the First World War there were four main classes of motor cars to be seen on the roads of Britain: the luxury limousine or landaulette, the not-so-dignified car with similar body design, the fairly high-powered open tourer—which usually combined grace of line with good performance—and the new-style "light" cars, which took their place on the road alongside the ten-year-old racing phaetons and two-seater voiturettes, which were still doing wonderful work among the medical profession.

But the advent of the lighter and easier-to-handle motor car was due to other causes than those of initial cost and running expenses, for private motoring was very largely an imported pastime, and though the French *Routes Nationales* were straight and high-speed driving was fairly safe, the narrow roads of England were fraught every mile with lurking dangers which made the smaller car far more suit-

Light Cars

The pre-First World War Standards and Singers were both well in the vanguard of light-car design, the latter make being the first vehicle of its kind to appear on the English market, which showed that it was possible to build a well-designed small car on large-car lines; and it is not surprising, therefore, that it boasted several novel features, including the combination of the gear-box with the back axle—an arrangement which considerably simpli-

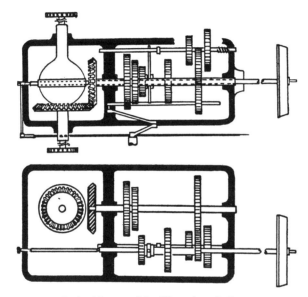

Panhard-Levassor "Crash" gearbox of 1890

able. High hedges, sudden corners and narrow village streets, with children playing in the road, were not conductive to peace of mind when driving a high-powered motor car in those days, and so the light car became increasingly popular in England and many new firms were created for its manufacture, with new ideas for cars built along the lines of larger vehicles instead of being not much more than glorified four-wheeled motor cycles—as were the ubiquitous cycle-cars of the time.

fied chassis design, though increasing the unsprung weight. But in their day the little Singer light cars were always well to the fore in road competitions. In the Royal Automobile Club trials at Harrogate and in the gruelling Austrian Alpine Tour they put up a marvellous performance, being, in fact, one of the most successful Edwardian light cars ever produced. This first type was ultimately developed by 1932 into the very popular "Junior" 8-h.p. Singer, which had an 848-c.c. engine capable of giving a

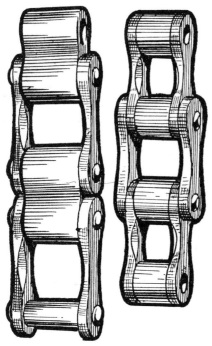

Early transmission chains
(Left) *Block chain.* (Right) *Brampton roller chain*

whole—a movement which, in the 1910s, even had its own magazine, the *Cycle-car*, of which the 80,000 copies sold of the first number showed only too clearly the interest of the public in its development.

So by the outbreak of the First World War an element of certainty was slowly but surely creeping into motoring. In France, where no less than twenty-three famous motor-car factories stretched along the banks of the Seine from Courbevoie to Billancourt, the roads of the surrounding countryside were freely used by manufacturers to put their finished products through their paces before delivery. Reputable makes, such as Panhard-Levassor, Renault, Mors, Sizaire, Charron, Delaunay-Belleville, Bayard-Clement, Delage, Hispano-Suiza, and Gobronne-Brillie, often spent more time on car-testing than they did on assembling, 200-mile road tests being quite usual if the test driver wasn't satisfied with a car's performance. Gear-boxes would often be taken down six or seven times before the chief examiner would pass them, and then, likely as not, after a sweetly-running car had been made many firms would order it to be stripped down, examined again, and reassembled before passing it into the customers' hands—a striking contrast to our modern methods, where purchasers often find the weak points in a car's design at their own cost and personal inconvenience.

Conversely, in England by 1912 the unpredictability of the results of the many public motor-car reliability trials was beginning to be realised by manufacturers, some of whom were content to rest on their laurels and hesitated to risk their reputation on such hazards, wherein standard cars were tested under straight-forward road-touring conditions. There seemed too much likelihood that new or lesser-known firms' products might be brought into equal or greater eminence,

top speed of about 55 m.p.h., with a petrol consumption of over forty miles per gallon.

Many of the first light cars had their genesis in the cycle-car—in fact, such light cars as the G.N., the Morgan and the A.C., in their original versions, were cycle-cars, which, but for the early mass-production methods which were beginning to appear in larger car design, might have developed into something more permanent. As it was, many cycle-cars were badly-designed, poorly-built vehicles, some of which were "back-yard" efforts designed and built by amateurs with a mechanical bent; and it was largely because of this that the cycle-car, as a definite type of motor car, never fulfilled its early promise to become an important part of Britain's motor industry. Too many thoroughly bad cycle-cars dealt the death-blow to the movement as a

Early transmission chain: Renolds silent chain

and it was undoubtedly due to this fact that the famous Scottish Reliability Trials, which had ceased in 1909, were never recommenced.

But manufacturers were loath to depart from traditional design, even though their cars' breed would have been improved by so doing, but the tiller steering and wick-carburettors of the Lanchesters, the rear-of-engine radiators of the Renaults, Charrons and Chenard-Walckers and the front-of-engine flywheels of the Napiers were all traditions of design which eventually died a slow death in face of the onslaught of improvement, progress and cheapness of production. Unfortunately, however, the economic conditions brought about by two world wars have made it impossible for the car purchaser to reap the reward of progress and improvement, for though production methods have cheapened beyond belief, the "£100" motor-car is today just a fantastic dream—incapable of ever becoming a reality, as it was once, as we shall see.

11·9 Albert coupé of 1919

CHAPTER VII

Small Beginnings of Famous Firms

IN THE year 1907 the Brooklands motor-racing track was opened, and from the very beginning of its career it assumed international fame. Three weeks after it was opened S. F. Edge, in his famous six-cylinder Napier, set up a new twenty-four-hour record by driving single-handed throughout and covering 1,581¼ miles at an average speed of 65 m.p.h. for twenty-four hours. Special lights were placed round the perimeter of the track for the night portion of the race, and two other Napiers, driven by teams of drivers, accompanied Edge on his epic run, which at the time was deemed impossible.

Cadillac cars, too, had undergone a remarkable interchangeability test at Brooklands during which they had been driven there from London and dismantled down to the last screw, the parts mixed up, and then quickly reassembled and raced for 500 miles on the track (without any special tuning up) by that doyen of motor-car driving, F. S. (Fred) Bennett.

Brooklands

For more than thirty years Brooklands was the mecca of the world of motor sport and a testing-ground for the British cars, which gained their share of the world's speed records when they competed with foreign models in speed events. Moreover, some of the more spectacular overseas racing events which were won because of previous experimental runs on Brooklands added a new lustre to the name of British motor cars. The triumph of the Sun-beams in the 3-litre section of the Dieppe Grand Prix of 1913 is an example; Sunbeams took first, second, and third places, achieving an average speed of 65 m.p.h. over a course of 956 miles.

Similarly, A. J. Hancock, in a 20-h.p. Vauxhall, set up a world record for 50 miles in 31 minutes at an average speed of just over 97 m.p.h. He also took the 21-h.p. class record for the "flying half-mile" at 101¼ m.p.h. and the "flying mile" at 99¾ m.p.h., eventually creating a new world record for the kilometre at 101½ m.p.h.

Vauxhalls were often competing fiercely with Darracqs and Sunbeams in those days, but none the less the 25-h.p. car designed by Laurence Pomeroy in 1913 broke eleven world records and a further fifteen class records; this was the famous Vauxhall "30/98"—a car upon which much has been written, especially as regards its popular name.

It has been said that it was neither a 30-h.p. nor a 98-h.p. car, but it is interesting to note that its horse-power at Shelsey Walsh in 1920 was given as 29·47. In point of fact "30/98" was the name given to it when some now-forgotten Vauxhall technician decided that 30 would be its brake horse-power at 1,000 r.p.m. and 98 its maximum brake horse-power. From the day of its first success at Wadding-ton Fells it became known as the "30/98".

Then in February, 1913, Percy Lambert became the first man to cover 100 miles in an hour when, driving a 25-h.p.

40-50 h.p. Rolls-Royce motor car of 1908

White steam car of 1903

VETERAN CAR BONNETS AND RADIATORS

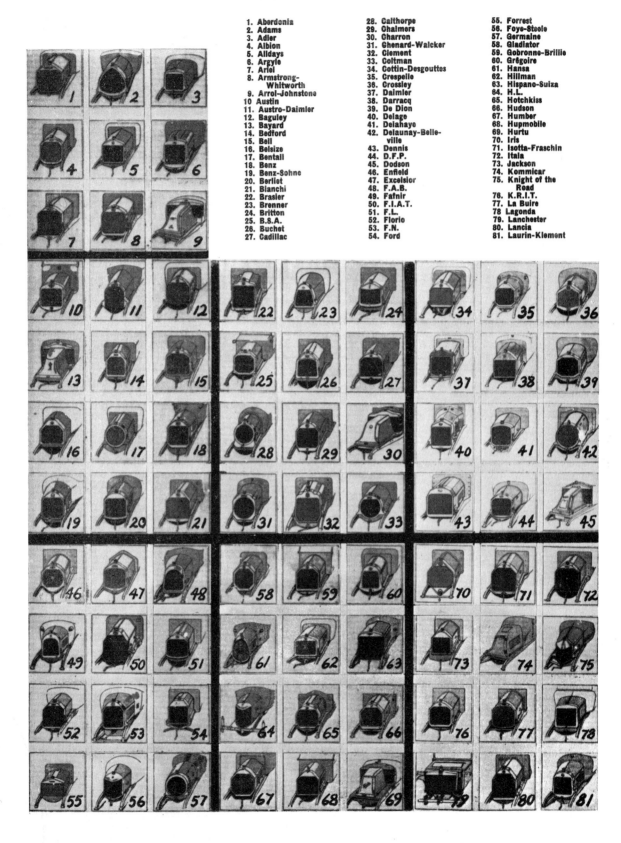

1. Aberdonia
2. Adams
3. Adler
4. Albion
5. Alldays
6. Argyle
7. Ariel
8. Armstrong-Whitworth
9. Arrol-Johnstone
10 Austin
11. Austro-Daimler
12. Baguley
13. Bayard
14. Bedford
15. Bell
16. Belsize
17. Bentall
18. Benz
19. Benz-Sohne
20. Berliet
21. Bianchi
22. Brasier
23. Brenner
24. Britton
25. B.S.A.
26. Buchet
27. Cadillac

28. Calthorpe
29. Chalmers
30. Charron
31. Ghenard-Walcker
32. Clement
33. Coltman
34. Cottin-Desgouttes
35. Crespelle
36. Crossley
37. Daimler
38. Darracq
39. De Dion
40. Delage
41. Delahaye
42. Delaunay-Belleville
43. Dennis
44. D.F.P.
45. Dodson
46. Enfield
47. Excelsior
48. F.A.B.
49. Fafnir
50. F.I.A.T.
51. F.L.
52. Florio
53. F.N.
54. Ford

55. Forrest
56. Foye-Steele
57. Germaine
58. Gladiator
59. Gobronne-Brillie
60. Grégoire
61. Hansa
62. Hillman
63. Hispano-Suiza
64. H.L.
65. Hotchkiss
66. Hudson
67. Humber
68. Hupmobile
69. Hurtu
70. Iris
71. Isotta-Fraschin
72. Itala
73. Jackson
74. Kommicar
75. Knight of the Road
76. K.R.I.T.
77. La Buire
78 Lagonda
79. Lanchester
80. Lancia
81. Laurin-Klement

VETERAN CAR BONNETS AND RADIATORS

82. Leon Bollee
83. La Licorne
84. Lorley
85. Lorraine-Dietrich
86. M.A.F.
87. Marathon
88. Martini
89. Mass
90. Mathis
91. Maudslay
92. Maxwell
93. Mercedes
94. Metallurgique
95. Miesse
96. Minerva
97. Mitchell
98. Mors
99. Motobloc
100. N.A.G.
101. Napier
102. Nazzaro
103. N.B.
104. N.S.U.
105. Opel
106. Oryx.
107. Overland
108. Paige
109. Palladium

110. Panhard
111. Pearson-Cox
112. Peugeot
113. Phoenix
114. Piccard-Pictet
115. Pick
116. Pilain
117. Pilot
118. Pipe
119. R.C.H.
120. Renault
121. Riley
122. R.M.C.
123. Rolls-Royce
124. Rover
125. S.A.V.A.
126. S.C.A.R.
127. S.C.A.T.
128. Scout
129. Schneider
130. Sheffield-Simplex
131. Siddeley-Deasey
132. Singer
133. Sirron
134. Sizaire-Berwick
135. Sizaire-Naudin
136. S.P.A.
137. Springuel

138. Spyker
139. Standard
140. Stanley
141. Star
142. Stoddard
143. Stoewer
144. Stoneleigh
145. Straker Squire
146. Studebaker
147. Sunbeam
148. Swift
149. Talbot
150. Thornycroft
151. Turcat-Mery
152. Turner
153. Unic
154. Valveless
155. Vauxhall
156. Vinot
157. Vivinius
158. Vulvan
159. Waverley
160. White
161. Wingfield
162. Withers
163. Wolseley
164. Zedel
165. Zebra

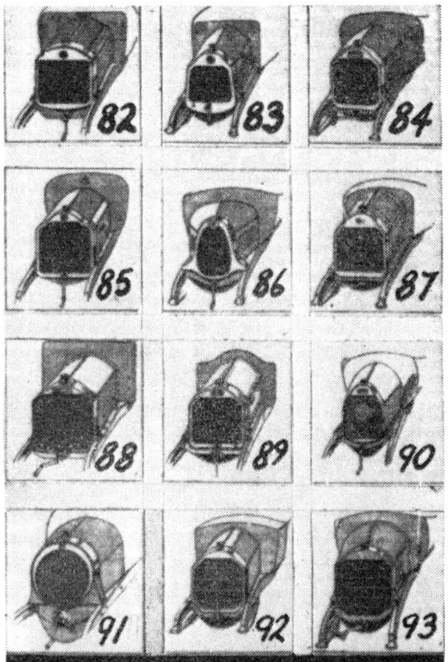

Model " B " Ford motor car of 1905

8-9 *h.p. Single-cylinder Chenard-Walcker car——*1908

Talbot, he travelled 103¼ miles in sixty minutes, a record which was broken in October that year by the ace French driver Jean Chassagne in a Sunbeam. Lambert tried again a week or so later, but he was killed at Brooklands in a brave attempt to regain the speed record.

With the opening of Brooklands, the famous Tourist Trophy Races, after so glorious a beginning, ceased; but they were resumed in 1914, when Kenelm Lee Guinness, whose name is perpetuated by the K.L.G. sparking-plug, won in a Sunbeam. Incidently, the success of the Sunbeam—and other later successes of these fine cars—was largely due to a naturalized Frenchman, Louis Coatalen, who joined the Crowden Motor Car company in 1900. He was chief engineer to Humber, and was William Hillman's partner when the Hillman-Coatalen car was designed in 1908, before he joined the Sunbeam Company.

During the two years immediately before the outbreak of the First World War achievement and expansion in the motor-car industry were in full stride. The failure of the cycle-car movement to establish itself as part of the industry left the way open for the development of such light cars as the Wolseley "Stellite", the Hillman, and the friction-driven G.W.K. There was progress everywhere, some firms progressing more quickly than others. Lanchesters cautiously concentrated on one or two models which were more or less improvements or variants of their earlier types, many of their modifications and minor developments being taken as forerunners of future standard practice. Their 20- and 28-h.p. cars, for example, were the first in Britain to incorporate high-pressure lubrication; moreover; they had pre-selector gear-change on all gears.

Similarly, the cars made by Crossley included such advanced features as four-wheel brakes, high-compression engines and electric lighting sets with the dynamo driven from the clutch-shaft. And that was in 1910!

Austin

By 1911 Austin were producing no fewer than six different horse-power models. As something of an indication of future trend of design which was not fully appreciated at the time, the world-famous Austin "Seven" was introduced in 1910. This was not yet the "Baby" Austin which was to prove the turning-point in the fortunes of that company, but it was the birth of the "baby car" idea in Great Britain—an idea which had its inception in the French "Baby Peugeot" of 1902.

The Austin "Seven" of 1910 and the "Baby Peugeot" of 1902 form an interesting comparison, for they had many points in common, in spite of the eight years' difference in their age. They were both two-seater voiturettes with single-cylinder engines, the former being a 6·8-h.p. with 4-in. bore and 5-in. stroke, and the latter a 5-h.p. with 3¹¹⁄₁₆-in. bore and stroke. Both had wooden wheels and shaft drive, but the Peugeot boasted steering-column gear-change—not such a modern development, after all!

Herbert Austin—later Lord Austin—emigrated to Australia as a youth, and there joined the Wolseley Sheep-shearing Company. In 1893 he returned to England and designed his first car—a three-wheeler—for the Wolseley Company, but in 1905 he started making his own cars at Longbridge, the first being known as the "25/30". This began a long line of productions which gained a fine reputation for long service and reliability.

Ford

The year 1912 was a very decisive one

in British progress towards the production of a "people's car"—towards the idea of a garage to every home and a car in every garage. It had long been realised that there was a market in Britain for a cheap-priced but good-quality car; indeed, the Ford Motor Car Company of the United States were already selling such vehicles in Britain through agents, and in 1912 they challenged British home industry by opening an assembly factory at Trafford Park, Manchester.

The world-famous Model "T" Ford was already an established favourite in America, and by 1912 was setting up a lusty challenge in Britain, over 3,000 being sold in the years 1910-11, and the Ford stand at the 1912 British Motor Show exhibiting a model which cost only £133 complete and "ready for the road"! The Ford was in Britain to stay, but although the Ford organisation was to grow to a vast concern and become part of Britain's motor-car industry, it was to have worthy rivals in the race to produce the "people's car"; and one of these rivals was William Richard Morris—later Sir William Morris and still later Lord Nuffield.

Morris

Morris started his business career at the age of sixteen with a capital of £4, setting up as a cycle agent and maker in Oxford, and, after graduating through motor-cycle production, in 1912 built his first car, which he called a Morris "Oxford". He was in no hurry to join in the motor-car production rush of the early years of the 1900s, but quietly watched the efforts of car-manufacturers and their customers' reactions to the cars they produced. He watched the cycle-car come into being and pass out of the British market and, like Austin, appreciated the need for a really good, cheap, popular car.

The 1912 Morris "Oxford" was introduced to the British public the following year at a price of £165: 400 cars were made, and the business expanded until, in common with most other motor-car manufacturing concerns, it was halted by the First World War, which nearly dealt the death-blow to the private car-making industry. So from modest beginnings in the cycle shop at Cowley Morris's organisation expanded steadily until the Morris "Cowley" was produced at the magic price of £100.

The secret of Morris's success was value for money. By advanced production methods, he was enabled to reduce his prices drastically just at the time when those of other cars were rising, and the £100 Morris "Cowley", with its famous "bull-nosed" radiator, was undoubtedly one of the most important factors in enabling the family man of small means to take up motoring for business and pleasure.

In an age when motor-car manufacture is becoming more and more concentrated in the hands of vast corporations, there are but few of the original veteran car-makers who are still with us. So it may be interesting to take a look at some of those firms which have survived—either completely or to some extent—the amalgamations of the past years, and have not disappeared or switched their activities into other lines of engineering business.

The A.C. Company commenced operations with a small three-wheeled commercial vehicle called the "Auto-carrier" (hence the firm's name), and in 1909 made its first passenger model, the "A.C." tricar, which boasted a single-cylinder 5½-h.p. engine and chain-drive to an epicyclic two-speed gear located in the single rear wheel. The price of the tricar was £90, but if one had desires for additional comfort a hood could be purchased for an additional 6 guineas;

side-lamps for 35s. a pair, a bulb horn for 15s. 6d., a windscreen for 2 guineas, and side aprons for 15s. Front-wheel brakes cost an extra 3 guineas and a Cowey speedometer £5—a rather striking comparison to the equipment included in the purchase price of the modern car.

Just before the First World War a four-wheeled car was produced which appeared again in 1919 with an Anzani four-cylinder engine, but ultimately a six-cylinder engine was designed with a light-alloy cylinder block which has remained the basic A.C. power unit ever since, for early use was made by this company of light metals for both main components and bodywork panelling. The man responsible for everything mechanical in the first "Autocarrier"—John Weller, one of the founders of A.C.—designed the Weller car which was exhibited at the 1903 Motor Show at the Crystal Palace and was of extremely advanced design, with its low-mounted radiator somewhat reminiscent of the present-day American practice.

Another motor-car firm still with us is Armstrong-Siddeley, which is one of the oldest companies, dating back as it does to 1902, when J. D. Siddeley—later Lord Kenilworth—founded the Siddeley Autocar Company. His early work resulted in the production of the Wolseley-Siddeley car, and then the Siddeley-Deasy—with either 18/24-h p. four cylinder or 30/36-h.p. six-cylinder engines, all of which cars contrast greatly to the firm's modern luxurious "Sapphires".

The history of the now-famous Aston-Martin Company began with a small, fast sports car made by Robert Bamford and Lionel Martin just before the First World War—a car which was put into production just after the Armistice and achieved immediate racing success. Aston-Martin's later successes are outside the period under review, for the firm can hardly be called makers of veteran cars!

Daimler, as we have already seen, were the first British car-manufacturers, the company being incorporated in 1896 and starting business in Coventry, using the patents of the original Daimler Company of Germany. The Royal Warrant was

Richardson light car

received in 1901, and for many years Daimler held the virtual monopoly in the supply of cars for the British Royal Family, whilst in their search for silence they adopted the Knight sleeve-valve engine, though improvements in orthodox valve gear ultimately resulted in a return to poppet valves. But Daimler's greatest contribution to the evolution of the motor car is undoubtedly their decision to adopt the fluid flywheel and epicyclic self-changing gear-box—the forerunner of our modern automatic transmissions as used chiefly in the United States.

The name of the H.R.G. Company is derived from the initials of H. R. Godfrey, an associate of A. Frazer-Nash in the G.N. cycle-cars of pre-First World War days, and that is the firm's main link with veteran days, for H.R.Gs. were not produced as such until 1935, with Meadows and, later, Singer engines.

Humber

Humber, one of the oldest companies in the industry, like many other firms, began by making bicycles, having been founded in 1867 by Thomas Humber. Thirty-two years, however, were to elapse before the first motor car to bear that famous name appeared. It was a single-cylinder model of 3½ h.p. Originally small and medium-sized cars were built, ranging from the tiny "Humberette" to the 30-h.p. six-cylinder model of 1908-9, nineteen different models being produced between 1906 and 1912 at prices ranging from £190 to £575.

As for the Jowett, the first prototype car was produced by the brothers Benjamin and William Jowett in 1906, after five years of experimental work, but it was not until 1910 that production of the later famous twin-cylinder, horizontally-opposed engine commenced. This was installed in a rugged chassis to power a

popular little car on which one could motor in those days for less than 1d. a mile. The original twin-cylinder models had a continual run of successes until the first four-cylinder car, with its horizontally-opposed engine, appeared in 1936.

Another of the motor-car firms which started life as bicycle manufacturers are Lea-Francis, which company was formed in 1896 and produced their first car in 1902—a 15/20-h.p. model. It was not, however, until well ahead of veteran days that the firm really made a name for itself, when the 10-h.p. car was made in 1922 and eventually became the first British motor car to be fitted with a supercharger and sold to the public as the "Supercharged Hyper-Sports" model.

Lagonda's history started when Wilbur Wright of Lagonda Creek, U.S.A., built his first motor vehicle—a tricar. That was in 1898, and eleven years were to elapse before the first car was made. Almost unbelievably, the combined body-chassis assembly was of steel—anticipating the present-day unit construction devoid of a regular chassis. Another interesting light car was produced in 1913—an 11-h.p. four-cylinder model which makes an interesting comparison with the big, fast Lagondas of later years. It too had its body and frame pressed from sheet metal in a single unit so designed as to provide support for engine and gear-box, yet today, oddly enough, Lagonda now build on elegant modern lines, using traditional coachbuilding methods, their car bodies being fabricated with aluminium panels mounted on wooden framework.

The Morgan Company has a long history, beginning as it did in 1909, when H. F. S. Morgan made motoring history by introducing his three-wheeled car, which he built in his garage at Malvern, in Worcestershire, for his own amusement, not as a commercial proposition. It was

200 h.p. four-cylinder "Blitzen Benz" of 1911

powered by a 7-h.p. twin-cylinder, air-cooled J.A.P. (John A. Prestwich Co.) engine, which was mounted in front and drove the single rear wheel by chain through the simplest type of transmission. A single-seater, it was shown at the 1911 Motor Cycle Exhibition, where it was much admired, but failed to be a success until it was re-designed as a two-seater, when immediate success followed and continued. Today the Morgan Company

but gradually British components began to be used; until recently they were fitted with British tyres and electrical equipment, and were finished in keeping with British ideas. The French Renault concern has been nationalised since the Second World War.

Rolls-Royce

The late Sir Henry Royce entered into partnership with the Hon. C. S. Rolls—

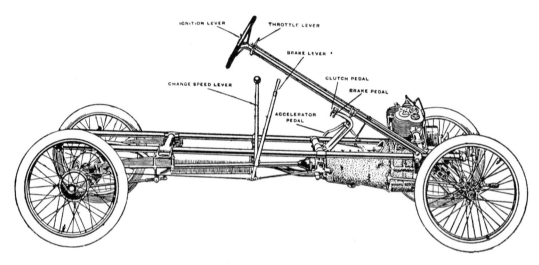

Typical light-car chassis of 1914

makes four-wheeled cars at Malvern, but it has never pursued an expansionist policy, and still occupies a small works where the cars are virtually hand-made. Incidentally, the simple sliding-pillar, independent front suspension of the three-wheelers is still used on Morgan sports cars.

The British subsidiary of the Renault Company was founded in 1905, the parent company being one of the pioneers of the French motor-car industry. Originally the British company simply assembled cars from parts sent over from France,

of early motor-racing fame—in December, 1904, a Royce car being used publicly from London to Margate and back earlier that year. It was an ideal combination of supreme designer and supreme demonstrator which brought the world-famous firm of Rolls-Royce into existence. The earlier types of cars achieved some notable successes, as, for instance, when a 20-h.p. four-cylinder model won the Tourist Trophy and subsequently established a new five-miles' record for petrol motor cars of 60 h.p. or less at Ormond Beach in Florida. But soon the entire energies of the Rolls-Royce works were centred upon the production of the fabulous 40/50 h.p. "Silver Ghost"—a superb six-cylinder machine which had immediate success as a touring car and established the fame of the company, and retained its position at the head of the world's cars until it was replaced by the "New Phantom" in 1925. During the First World War some highly successful armoured cars were produced by the company on standard "Silver Ghost" chassis, and when the Commander-in-Chief of the British Army landed in France in August, 1914, he was conveyed in a Rolls-Royce "Silver Ghost"—not mounted on the more historic battle charger!

The inception of the Rover Company dates back to 1877, when W. Sutton and J. K. Starley began building penny-farthing "bone-shaker" bicycles in Coventry. The original Rover Company was formed in 1896, and seven years later they produced their first motor vehicle, a $2\frac{1}{4}$-h.p. motor-cycle, which was followed the next year by an 8-h.p. single-cylinder car. The Singer Company was also established in Coventry the year previous to the start of Rover, and also for the manufacture of bicycles. Later, like Rover, they next made motor cycles, and finally entered the car field to later produce the famous Singer light car, which we have already noticed.

Standards, on the other hand, entered the car-manufacturing business without any previous experience in the cycle or motor-cycle fields when they produced in 1903 a little 6-h.p. single-cylinder model with a three-speed gear-box and shaft drive. Several very successful family touring cars and light cars followed, all of which are easily recognisable by the characteristic shouldered radiator and Union Jack badge. (It was, unfortunately, illegal to use the Royal Standard, as was originally intended.)

The Sunbeam-Talbot Company of to-day has its roots in the Sunbeam Motor Car Company of Wolverhampton, which built their first car in 1899, and the Clement-Talbot Company, which was itself an amalgamation of the Clement and Talbot companies. In point of fact, the first Sunbeam car was actually built by Messrs. John Marston Ltd., who previously made Sunbeam bicycles and later made even the sparking plugs for the newly-founded motor company. What car-builder today makes his own sparking plugs?

Although at the time the horizontal engine was all the fashion, the first Sunbeam was equipped with a vertical single-cylinder engine of 6 nominal h.p. with an exposed crankshaft, like a gas engine. The engine had electric ignition instead of the then popular "hot-tube" type, and though it had solid rubber tyres, was proudly of wholly British make—which was saying something in those days!

Triumphs, too, had their origin in the bicycle business—also in Coventry, where they started business in 1885, later to expand into the motor-cycle field, and not entering the car market until after the First World War with tourers and light cars.

CHAPTER VIII

Motoring at Sixteen Pence per Mile

IN THE years immediately before the outbreak of the First World War—the
peak years of veteran car perfection—
there was a sense of sport and fun about
motoring that is almost absent today.
Happy days they were; heroic days of
the little single-cylinder racing phaetons,
when on the country roads of England the
motor car was something of a rare visitor,
and even in London the traffic was about
equally divided between mechanically-
and horse-drawn vehicles.

Motor cars unpredictably often broke
down, and the mysteries of electricity as
applied to them was only dimly understood, the elusive current sometimes giving
out completely without any warning, or
persisting in taking a fiendish delight in
deliberately missing the sparking plugs
and causing the engine to stop. It was
even not outside the bounds of possibility
for a high-tension cable to leak to the
steering column and the current find its
was to the chassis by way of the astonished
driver's hands and body!

Motoring in those far-off days was
something of a fair-weather sport, for

drizzling rain and a strong head wind
could make driving almost impossible.
It was a case of pulling one's cap well
down over one's eyes, going easy, and
hoping for the best—particularly at night,
when one always drove close to the near-
side gutter and kept a sharp look-out for
walkers, horsemen and farm wagons,
which often used to wander all over the
road.

In those days, too, roadside troubles
presented a very real problem. Garages
were few and far between, and if the
motorist knew nothing about his car and
how it worked, he was likely to be stuck
for hours before he could get a lift or a tow
to the nearest town.

Sometimes the oddest of breakdowns
would bring a car to a standstill. Sharp
edges on the metal tubing of the water-
cooling system were often prone to cut
into the rubber-pipe connections and thus
cause the engine to seize up through lack
of water. Brake shoes would wander off
the rear-wheel brake drums when the
brakes were applied in an emergency, and
a lamp-post or a telegraph pole bring the

day's adventures to an abrupt end! Dirt and water in the carburettor due to the absence of a petrol filter could cause ear-splitting backfires, and a fierce clutch cause the car to leap suddenly forward with a lurch which almost back-somer-saulted the unfortunate driver into the rear seats—if there were any! If not, he went into the road! On such occasions the steel-studded back tyres would rip mercilessly round, striking showers of sparks from the flint road to the accompaniment of the pungent smell of burning rubber, the heat often scalping the tyre of its steel-studded leather skin.

Such fierce clutches, which were either really "in" or really "out", gave the driver of those days very little or no finesse of control when changing gears—an operation which needed no small courage on his part to perform. It was then a highly

involved and much-dreaded manœuvre, and it was something of a trick of the trade to apply neatsfoot oil to the leather face of a fierce clutch to make it easier and powdered fuller's earth if it slipped too much.

Looking back, one can but feel admiration for those veteran cars and respect for the adventurous men who drove them, dealing with explosions and grinding gears, lurchings and skiddings, all so ludicrously serious then, but so understandable now that their true causes are known. But it must not be thought that such high motoring adventure persisted until after the First World War, for by then refinements were beginning to be incorporated and general design to become more settled down into more or less that which continued—with minor modifications—until the middle 1930s.

The man who motored in the first decade of this century learnt his lessons at the rough school of trial and error, and usually paid a very high price for the experience he bought. Instruction manuals were virtually non-existent and text-books about motoring were few, those published seldom dealing with one's own particular make of car. Most motorists had their own list of "hints and tips"—and carried it under their hat! They had their own ideas as to how a repair should be done—and did it themselves! They made up their own anti-freeze radiator mixtures of one-third glycerine and two-thirds water; they used

a reeking concoction of castor oil and fuller's earth for a slipping clutch; and cleaned rain-spotted paintwork with equal parts of vinegar, linseed oil and methylated spirits.

Comfort

They believed in as much comfort as possible, too, when motoring—inexpensive comfort, such as folded brown paper under their coats! They found that it was absolutely windproof and retained body heat in an extraordinary manner. None the less, there would usually be an odd spare overcoat or two in the rear tonneau of a four-seater car which would come in very useful on a long night ride. Coachman's waterproof gloves and snow-boots were also much used until the days when celluloid side-screens and wind-screens made such garb unnecessary.

The mention of night riding brings us to lamps—not the slick electric lamps one can switch on and off without leaving the driving seat, but oil and acetylene gas ones which needed constant care and

attention, for a faulty oil rear-lamp could give expensive trouble by going out unknown to the driver and thus doubling the cost of a journey by incurring a heavy fine for not "showing a red light to the rear"!

Good drivers were meticulous about their lamps—particularly acetylene head-lamps, of which the diameter could be anything up to 15 in. They were kept safely protected from mud and dust during the daytime by wrapping them in moleskin-lined waterproof canvas bags which could be bought for the purpose. Such lamps were not too expensive, but they were vital to the driver who used his car during the hours of darkness, and after a night journey, no matter at what hour he arrived home, the sensible motorist's first job would be to open up the acetylene generator and wash out its carbide container in a bucketful of water, bringing it into the house if there was the slightest sign of frost, so that the water in it did not freeze and burst the container. Incidentally, acetylene generators never

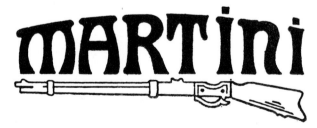

froze while working, due to the heat generated when the water contacted the carbide.

As we have seen, it was around the 1908 period that the evolution of the small, 10/15-h.p. motor-car became the natural development, for it was rapidly becoming obvious that but few people could afford the upkeep of a big, heavy car. Consider the expenses account of an actual veteran motorist of 1907 who owned a 16/20-h.p. four-seater Humber:

	£	s.	d.
Original cost of car with five tyres	625	0	0
Selling price of car . .	300	0	0
Depreciation (7¾d. per mile)	325	0	0
Petrol (730 gallons—1d. per mile)	44	0	11
Lubricating oil (¼d. per mile)	9	12	1
Repairs not covered by insurance	21	10	10
Insurance, registration, licences, number-plates .	19	6	6
Head-lamps (extra) . .	14	0	0
Compensation to cyclist in accident . . .	5	0	0
Tyre retreading and repairs .	116	2	0
Sundries and cleaning materials . . .	5	2	5
Chauffeur's wages and travelling expenses . . .	118	5	3
Total (9,900 miles at 1s. 4d. per mile) . . .	£678	10	0

Considering that today the approximate cost of running a car works out somewhere in the region of 5d. per mile, it is no small wonder that greater attention was beginning to be given to the unloaded weight of motor cars. More tare weight meant the provision of more powerful engines, more wear and tear, and less carrying capacity, so some designers slowly began to realise that it was better to use engines with six small cylinders than with four large ones. But even so there was a revival of the old two-cylinder engine, which was due in no small measure to the amazing success and development of the motor-cab—or taxi-cab, as we now call it—and this being so, quite naturally the makers of these vehicles, such as Renault, used the same engines for their smaller private cars and light runabouts.

By 1908, too, motoring was getting more comfortable, for it was beginning to be recognised that a motor car must be usable at all seasons—a matter which received much more attention at the time on the Continent than it did in Great Britain. Noiselessness and lack of vibration were beginning to be sought after, and the "high-speed racing phaeton" was slowly ceasing to have quite the charm it used to have for the average motorist, who wanted a more comfortable vehicle

with a speed of about 20 m.p.h., side doors, and some sort of hood or top covering which could be raised or lowered at will. The "saloon" car had not, of course, arrived on the scene.

Noise

One of the most interesting attempts of the day at producing a motor car which was free of noise and shock was undoubtedly the Rolls-Royce eight-cylinder landaulette, which, as early as 1905, was produced as a challenge to the silent, electrically-driven town landaulettes which were so popular at the time.

The fact that this outstanding vehicle appeared more than a year before the six-cylinder 40/50-h.p. model which was to form the basis of the immortal Rolls-Royce "Silver Ghost", gives some idea of just how much ahead of its time the design really was—a "Vee-eight" engine with four blocks of two cylinders with gear-driven forced lubrication and fan cooling. And note the date, 1905!

But though silence was very costly in those far-off days, there were other car-manufacturing firms who were seeking the same objective along other lines of thought and design. As early as the first decade of the present century it was realised that most of the noise made by a motor car was caused by the gear-box, and though most makers eventually overcame the gear-noise bugbear by mechanical design, there were some who thought that they could get a more flexible and quieter drive by substituting an electrical coupling for the orthodox

gear-box initiated by Levassor—the *train balladeur*, as the French termed it.

One of the earliest motor cars built to operate on this petrol-electric system was a Belgian one produced at Liège—the "Automixte", which embodied the rather peculiar Henri-Pieper system and was capable of a speed of some 40 m.p.h. On this car, instead of the usual change-speed gears, a dynamo and accumulators were used, the 24-h.p. engine driving the armature of a dynamo, which in turn drove an electric motor connected to the rear wheels. When the load was light, part of the engine's power was used to charge the accumulators, and when the load was heavy the dynamo could be used as an electric motor to further assist in turning the road wheels—the current being suplied from the accumulators.

But although great things were claimed by the makers for the "Automixte", which gave excellent results and was very reliable and smooth to drive, the motor-car world of the day was against it, and continued to pin its faith on improved forms of mechanical gear-box transmission. Indeed, the non-acceptance of the unusual in all branches of engineering and transport will always be something of an enigma. However, the Henri-Pieper system reappeared several years later in a slightly modified form on the Tilling-Stevens motor-buses which faithfully served the public for many years on several routes of the London General Omnibus Company.

But to return to the motorist of the immediate pre-First World War days and the cars he drove, the subject of the tools carried is an interesting one, for the veteran motorist had to be very methodical in his motoring methods if he was to be sure of getting to his destination.

Tools

Motor-car tool kits carried aboard were perfect examples of forethought and kindness to tools such as is hardly known today among motorists, who, more often than not, pass their car to the nearest garage for servicing and overhaul. In those days, tools were generally carried in a neat leather roll and deposited in an oak or mahogany box on the nearside running board, and the contents of that box, apart from tools, bore eloquent witness to the possible eventualities of a motor-car journey at that time.

There was a special nipple to attach to the underside of the burner bracket of acetylene lamps, by which the tyre pump could be attached to blow out any blockages in the minute hole in the burner. Spare burners were also carried, and a couple of spare trembler blades for the vibrating-type ignition coils (unless a magneto ignition was fitted). For the carburettor, a spare needle valve, float, and balance arms were taken along, as well as a bottle of celluloid solution for repairing accumulator cases—which were then made of celluloid. Coils of copper wire, emery paper, valve springs, rubber tape, and a small sackful of dry sand for use in case of carburettor fires were also carried. Truly the motorist of those days, if he was sensible, was not going to be caught high and dry miles from the nearest garage! And garages in the early 1900s were few and far between!

Another interesting point about veteran motoring is that the tool-box and its contents were never sold with the car; nor were the lamps. These were duly unshipped when a car changed hands, and

remained with the owner for years; he mounted them proudly on whatever "ship of the road" he was running.

One always associated polished brasswork with veteran cars, and though on some of the veterans still with us this "brasswork" complex may seem to us to be rather overdone, it must be remembered that only on the "super-cars" of the day was nickel used for lamps and fitments; the majority of cars were literally things of sheerest beauty on which all metalwork—both that exposed to view and that under the bonnet—was kept brightly polished. Indeed, the measure of a good motorist was the measure of the gleaming brasswork of his car. The superb contrast between polished mahogany and burnished brasswork on a veteran has to be seen to be appreciated—in contrast to the dull, drab sleekness of our modern cars, which are by and large devoid of every embellishment, in the so-called interests of ease of cleaning.

The writer can well remember a 1910 35/40-h.p. Mercedes with its massive honeycomb radiator of resplendent brass and copper, its 12-in. acetylene headlamps, and starting-handle big enough for the two-handed grip necessary to start the engine, its deep-set, shining black mudguards, which one could have jumped on without fear of buckling them, and its luscious crimson-maroon bodywork and brass boa-constrictor horn; and the whole

body immaculately lined out in black and red with a care and precision unknown on present-day cars.

And as for driving such a car in the days when it was new, in summer, if goggles were not worn, one's eyes were made red and sore after a day's run by dust and flies, and many motorists used to carry a bottle of boracic lotion when motoring in summertime! Today such a precaution seems ridiculous, but we must remember that if a fly got in one's eye when one was travelling at 30 m.p.h. and one blinked, one had travelled 50 ft. with one's eyes shut, and a lot could happen in 50 ft. on a wet road without any front-wheel brakes! Truly, motoring in those days could be something of an adventure, even if it had its hardships.

It is often stated—and rightly so—that veteran motor cars were better built than those made to-day. There is a good reason for the difference, which is one of manufacturer's policy rather than their ability. Times have changed; the value of money has changed; and the ideas and ideals of prospective purchasers of motor cars have changed.

In the days before the First World War, a man about to buy a motor car would ask the very obvious question: "How long will it last?" It was a simple question, but one to which in those days there was no definite answer. It could not be stated that a motor car would wear out in the accepted sense any more than it could have been said that the average suit of clothes would wear out and become absolutely useless. The value of most articles in everyday use, even today, cannot be measured in terms of actual wearing capacity: appearance, fashion, general depreciation and cost of repairs all enter into the question.

In the case of motor cars back in the days when they were built to last, it was utterly impossible to assess the useful life of a well-built motor car. Most of it was virtually indestructible; only tyres, bearings, and moving parts subjected to continual wear and tear would wear out, and these were readily replaceable; so there was no good reason why a car should not last, to all intents and purposes, indefinitely. And many thousands of them did—as witness those which to-day take part in the London to Brighton Run.

To get this "better-made" problem in the right perspective, one must remember that in 1913, say, there were many thousands of motor cars in daily service which had been on the road for ten or fifteen years or more and had built up enormous mileages—far greater in many cases than our modern cars—through remaining in their original form. They were often hopelessly out-of-date, but their owners kept them running because they were

useful and did not wear out—appearance mattered but little, and it was often ignored.

So it was not, in those far-off days, a question of how well was a motor car made or how long would it last, but rather one of how long its owner desired to keep it—in view of the rapidity of change of mechanical design and performance. The same is true to-day, but for a different reason—the change of car fashion and "body-styling", not for any radical improvement in its fundamental mechanics. The car of 1910 did not look so hopelessly out-of-date by 1912, nor was one of 1912·considered very old-fashioned at the end of the First World War, during which but few new cars were available to the public. It must be remembered, too, that the rate of development of design was much faster then than it has been over the last twenty-five years, and whereas we today feel proud to drive a 1924 3-litre T.T. Sunbeam, the driver of 1914, however enthusiastic he might have been, would not have fancied driving about in a twenty-five-year-old Benz dog-cart! Times have changed.

Self Starters

Among the outstanding improvements which made their appearance in Great Britain immediately before the First World War was the self-starter, with which nearly half the motor-manufacturers in the United States had been fitting their cars for several years. As we have already seen, Ford and other American manu-

facturers were trying out the English market, and the sight of an English owner of one of their cars leisurely starting his engine without leaving the driving seat must have been annoying to the driver of an English car who had to struggle and sweat to "start on the handle", to the accompaniment of backfires and an occasional broken wrist!

The old "Cape-cart hood" was another item of comfort which was improved about that time, for it was a draughty affair at the best and side-curtains did not improve it greatly, as they only acted as air-scoops which effectively directed into the driver's face wind, rain and mud-splash from any car which chanced to be driving ahead. Indeed, in our snug modern saloon cars it is almost impossible for us to realise the appalling driving conditions of forty years ago.

Even a present-day run in the winter in a veteran car still does not rightly paint the picture, for the mud and slush on the roads of 1910 does not exist today—even on the most lonely of by-roads.

To scurry along into the teeth of a December south-westerly gale, flinging mud and water to left and right, deluged with rain and with one's clothes sticking to one's back, was indeed a hazardous adventure of which the modern motorist in his wind-tight, heated saloon car knows nothing. Yet without those grand old cars and their intrepid drivers we should not have our sleek and comfortable cars to-day. They were links in the chain of motor-car evolution.

CHAPTER IX

'Josephine' Rejuvenated

TWO DEVASTATING wars have taken place since the motor cars we now term "veteran" were running in their tens of thousands on the roads of Great Britain, America, and the European continent. Bombs have fallen, wrecking factories, museums and private garages where precious examples of old cars were stored. So it is not surprising that the tracking-down and finding of an unknown veteran car is today very unlikely, and the discoverer of such a vehicle, in almost any stage of decay, can consider himself very fortunate.

However, the writer's younger son did have the good fortune to find such a vehicle—the 6·99-h.p. racing phaeton Renault.

As purchased, the Renault—which has now been duly christened *Josephine*—consisted of a bare, rusty chassis, an engine and gear-box, a back and front axle, five rather decrepit wheels devoid of tyres, a battered bonnet and a leaky radiator, together with a couple of boxes full of odd bits and pieces, the majority of which were rusty beyond imagination.

This motley collection of motor car parts was duly loaded on to a lorry and brought home to be almost literally poured out on my garage floor just as winter was closing in, whilst I myself, though a motoring enthusiast, began to mildly chastise myself for being so romantic as to ever have condoned the purchase of such a load of "junk"! I surveyed that heap with very mixed feelings. Every-thing was rusty and bent, and what remained of the little car seemed to cry out for kindness and love—the touch of a hand that cared.

Then I began to realise that here before me was indeed the motor car of our wildest dreams, a veteran of the "Edwardian" period, loyal to its heritage and proud in its survival, a motor car to be cherished as a tangible relic of a more heroic motoring age. And that bent and rusty·heap of motor-car parts became the centre of attraction at my house for the next eighteen months, during which time the bits and pieces were sorted out and derusted, where necessary, with "Jenolite".

Time rolled on. Winter, spring and summer passed, and autumn was well on the way before much could be seen by way of rebuilding *Josephine*. It was a slow job which entailed not only the scrupulous cleaning and sorting out of every part, but a great amount of research work to achieve accuracy of body size and shape, for we had not the inclination to ruin such a lovely little chassis and engine by mounting a soap-box behind the 12-in. diameter steering-wheel and calling it a veteran motor car.

Bodywork

In this matter, a Renault catalogue of 1908, borrowed from the owner of a 38-h.p. Renault of the same period, helped immensely, and we felt that if the job was worth doing it was worth doing well, so

Clement-Talbot touring car of 1908

*The first Vauxhall motor car—*1903

Swing-seat 7 h.p. Alldays and Onions car of 1904

Rolls-Royce motor car of 1905

*The world-famous Ford Model " T "—*1908

Model " K " Ford motor car of 1907

A four-wheeled "Wind Wagon" shown at Brussels

"Coronation" Darracq of 1910

40 h.p. Daimler Landaulette of 1908

*60 **h.p.** Austin Phaeton of* 1908

Off-side view of 30-50 h.p. Armstrong-Whitworth engine of 1912

*Off-side sectional view of typical four-cylinder engine of
the First World War period*

*Near-side sectional view of typical four-cylinder engine of
the First World War period*

24 h.p. Sports Sunbeam—1919

Chassis of Wolseley-built experimental gyroscopic car 1912-14

26 h.p. de Dion open tourer of 1913

*" Prince Henry " Vauxhall—*1913

Three-seater Turcat-Mery of 1913

*Four-cylinder Arrol-Johnstone " Victory " model—*1918

Six-cylinder, two-seater, Grand Prix Napier of 1908

seasoned ash and birch were used for the body, with glue and screws in the approved coachbuilder's fashion. The body was built just as it would have been built by the craftsmen of fifty years ago—a craft which seems to have now almost completely disappeared from the realms of motor-car manufacture.

Yet it was a "labour of love" in which my two sons and I all took a hand, whilst on week-ends friends of the boys, hearing of our prize, would roll up and discuss motor body-building over endless mugs of hot coffee or limejuice—as the weather dictated! We had *Josephine* for every meal, and on occasions I found myself lying awake at night scheming up ideas for doing some particular job on the car. The project became almost an obsession with us—an enthusiasm which seemed to spread through the whole household!

The body, as has been mentioned, was hand-built from hardwood, which formed the structural framework, this being covered with mahogany-faced plywood and $\frac{1}{4}$-in.-thick mahogany sheeting, which was duly steamed to shape to produce the back of the seat. The whole wooden framework was, of course, constructed on an oblong basework which rested on and was bolted to the steel chassis to form a rigid foundation upon which to work. Then came the question of seat upholstery —which was a very real problem.

I had seen other veteran motor cars on which the excellent bodies built had been marred by upholstery of modern leather or one of the synthetic "leathers" so much in vogue today; so we felt that *Josephine* deserved better than this, but the question was where could really old leather be obtained—morocco leather by preference, as was used in the "good old days".

Upholstery

Months went by during which we all were on the look-out for such leather, without any success. Then a friend of one of our friends told us about some old horse-drawn landaus which were rotting away in a Kentish orchard, and, hot foot, we followed up the clue. There, sure enough, under the apple and plum trees were half a dozen half-a-century-old vehicles in various advanced stages of decay, their wheels almost axle-deep in mud and their proud old hardwood bodies swathed in brambles. An elder tree with a 5-in. thick trunk was growing through the spokes of one of the wheels, giving witness to their age.

For forty years the old coaches had been rooted in that orchard, pushed off the roads as unwanted by the very veteran motor cars we admired so much. Forty summers and forty winters these coach bodies had survived, and their wood joints were still materially intact and sound—defying the merciless onslaught of our hammers as we strove to remove carefully the leather and horse-hair from their seats. And, incredible though it may seem, that leatherwork still smelt like leather and was as supple as ever after all the merciless weathering it had received. And why? It was real morocco leather, tough, and tanned by real craftsmen—a credit to the tanner's art and a violent contrast to the synthetic makeshifts so prevalent on our modern cars.

So, much to the village yokels' amusement, the three of us staggered from the orchard to the station with arms bulging with horse-hair-filled upholstery, lengths of brass beading, brass door-handles, and various period bits and pieces, leaving a trail of stuffing to grace the railway carriage when we detrained at our home station! But we had got our morocco leather, and that was all that mattered.

All the materials were now to hand for the finishing-off of the body, and whilst

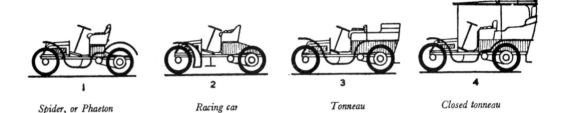

| *Spider, or Phaeton* | *Racing car* | *Tonneau* | *Closed tonneau* |

this was being done the chassis was taken in hand so that it could be ready to receive the body when the latter was completed. Firstly, every fitting that was bolted on to it was removed, leaving the bare chassis, which was first washed down with paraffin to remove all grease; then all traces of old paint and rust were scraped off and the whole treated to a thorough rubbing-down with sand-paper; and, finally, petrol was used to give a final perfect cleaning before the application of the paint under-coat.

During the scraping-down, some of the original grey chassis paint was discovered, so that colour was used for the re-painting, the very best "ordinary" undercoating and paint being used for the three coats given. Cellulose-type paints were not used, as it was desired to keep as truly to "period" techniques as possible. The outsides of the chassis, which could be seen when the body was in place, were finished in vermilion—unlined.

Springs

The front and rear springs were in rather a sorry state when we started work on them, but they were completely dismantled leaf by leaf and reassembled with grease after being painted where required—also vermilion. The steering-gear was also taken to pieces, scraped and degreased and painted the same colour, as was the back-axle casing, which latter had to be considerably repaired with new materials where rust had eaten completely through over $\frac{1}{8}$-in. of the axle casing on one side of the differential box. This job we incidentally had to get done at an engineering shop, but the fitting of the new casing was done at home with the aid of two blow-pipes and hours of patience.

As the shackle bolts between the springs and the chassis lugs were badly worn and irreplaceable, we took a hint from the method used on the old coaches in the orchard and used rubber bushes—a method which is wrongly supposed to be a modern invention: 2-in. pieces cut from the garden hose filled the bill to perfection!

The internals of the little twin-cylinder engine were fortunately found to be in excellent condition, the insides of the cylinder bores being polished like tubes of glass and unscored. The main and big-end bearings also needed no attention, as all the moving parts were of such ample robustness that nothing short of running without oil could possibly wreck anything. The massive gear-box, which we later found was the same type as that fitted by Renault's to their 1908 38-h.p. car, was also in perfect condition, the teeth on the second-gear pinions still showing the original milling marks made when they were machined! The clutch and carden shaft gave us no headaches either, it being merely a matter of removing age-hardened grease and oil and reassembling.

5	6	7	8
Tonneau de luxe	*Double phaeton*	*Closed phaeton*	*Brake, or Char-a-banc*

When the little two-seater body was completed after many months of working an unfamiliar material with unfamiliar tools, it was first given a coat of grey flattening paint and rubbed down with wet garnet-paper before stopping any cracks and proofing any knots. Then came the first colour coat—one of deep blue. This also was rubbed down in the same way, only to be followed by second, third, and fourth colour coats—each with its rubbing down.

Paintwork

The top coat presented quite a problem. It was essential that it was applied in a dust-free, warm atmosphere, so the body was placed on the chassis and the car rolled out into the open early one summer morning on to ground which had previously been gone over with a water-can. Fortunately, all went well, and by eight o'clock the same evening the drying off crisis had passed and *Josephine* was pushed back under cover for the night in all her deep-blue glory.

The following week-end, a signwriter friend had his skill and steady hand pressed into service to line the body out in vermilion, the felloes, spokes and naves of the wheels also being similarly treated. And, incidentally, it must be placed on record that we had to cut the rim of our fifth wheel to pieces to repair two of the others where they were com-pletely rotted away through standing on wet ground. That fifth wheel undoubtedly saved the situation!

In the meantime, the magneto had been dismantled and overhauled, as had the massive brass Renault carburettor, and at long last came the moment we had all been waiting so long for—the first trial of the engine.

With a tankful of petrol, lubricator tank full of Castrol S.A.E. 50, and the engine sump filled with a gallon of Castrol "R", the engine was "swung". The immediate result was a vicious back-fire—the ignition had been timed a wee bit too much "advanced". This was corrected, and on the next attempt she fired and the proud little engine was soon ticking over in fine style, to the accompaniment of a rousing cheer from the assembled crowd of friends who had come up specially to hear "what she sounded like".

Then with lubricator drip-feeds properly checked and working, my son hopped aboard, declutched, engaged first speed and tentatively let in the clutch. This was the moment we'd all been waiting two years for. The little car moved forward under her own steam, soon to disappear round the corner down the road in a swirling cloud of blue smoke— while we all cheered ourselves hoarse once again.

So ended the rebuilding of a veteran

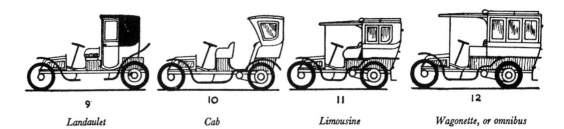

9	10	11	12
Landaulet	*Cab*	*Limousine*	*Wagonette, or omnibus*

motor car. It had been a long, tough job, but enthusiasm won out in the end; we had produced a motor car out of a heap of wreckage—a motor car we are proud to have in the family. And since her re-birth little *Josephine* has made two trips to Wales and back—each of well over 1,000 miles; and on neither trip did we even have to open the tool-box—which tool-box, incidentally, was equipped in the approved "veteran" fashion, even down to a 1907 edition of Macready's *Dictionary of Motoring*!

Your guess is as good as mine as to the real reason why my son and I suddenly decided to forsake the yearly Brighton Run of 100 miles and turn *Josephine*'s tiny bonnet towards the mountains of Wales.

Some friends envied us and said they would have given anything to have had the opportunity, while others shook their heads sympathetically and forthrightly pronounced us "a couple of lunatics"! But at all events *Josephine* merrily cantered to Wales and back, gamely hauling herself and about 24 stone of passengers and camping gear a round 1,000 miles, including the crossing of the Cambrian and Berwyn mountains on the way. Not so bad for a fifty-year-old motor car!

CHAPTER X

Driving a Veteran Car

IT IS strange to look back on the days when people did not know the difference between an exhaust pipe and a carburettor —did not, in fact, know the functions of a solitary one of the many curious things which were to be seen when the bonnet of a motor car was lifted. Today it is hard to realise that the majority of motoring enthusiasts of veteran days started their motoring knowledge and experience from scratch; perhaps finding some friend who by training or inclination was already something of an engineer who could help them on their quest for knowledge. Today all is different. Most people know something of the workings of a car, and there are many millions who can drive one. But even so, there are few who could get out of the driving seat of their streamlined saloon and settle down with confidence behind the steering wheel of a restored veteran motor car and drive it away. Veteran-car-driving is an art all of its own—an art which takes a deal of learning, unless, of course, the driver is a man old enough to have actually driven such a car and has graduated through the years. Such a man is the only qualified driving instructor when it comes to handling a veteran motor car. So let us see what the technique actually entails—in vivid contrast to the simplicity of modern driving.

Prior to starting, the driver should see that the engine sump contains the proper quantity of the right grade of oil, bearing in mind that too much oil will do very little damage to the engine, but too little oil will. The gear-box and rear-axle oil levels must also be checked, and all other moving parts of the car properly lubricated, grease cups and oil holes being topped up as and when required. The petrol tank must, of course, be filled, and on no account must a dirty stick or ruler be used for measuring the depth of petrol therein, for, due to the absence of a petrol filter between the tank and the carburettor on most veteran cars, any foreign matter in the tank will find its way to the carburettor and probably block its jet. The radiator tank must be filled with water—rain-water by preference—and the petrol tap between the petrol tank and the carburettor turned "on". The gear lever must be placed in "neutral" and the hand-brake, which locks the rear wheels, must be put "on".

Starting

If the engine has been cold for some time, it is advisable to give the starting handle a few turns with the throttle half open and the magneto or coil switched off, for this is better than flooding the car-burettor. After the preliminary "swing", switch on the magneto or ignition and grasp the starting handle loosely in the crooked palm of the hand, keeping the thumb on the same side of the handle as the fingers. This latter advice is very important, as the thumb can be dislocated or the wrist broken should the handle be gripped wrongly and the engine backfires.

A sharp upward pull should start the engine.

Now step to the side of the steering wheel and gently ease back the throttle pre-set lever until the engine settles down to a nice running speed, checking the drip-feed lubricators to see that each drip feed is delivering oil correctly to front and rear engine main bearings and to whatever other moving surfaces the lubricator caters for.

On getting into the driving seat, depress the left-hand (clutch) pedal to the full and rest the palm of the right hand on the head of the change-speed lever, moving the lever from "neutral" forward to "first-speed" position. The engagement of the gear will be apparent by a light "locking" sensation communicated to the driver's hand—a sensation difficult to describe, but soon intuitively recognised.

The first-speed being in mesh, the throttle (accelerator) pedal is now depressed, and when the engine has gathered some speed, the hand-brake is released and the clutch let in, the accelerator being depressed more and more until a balance of engine power to that required to move the car is obtained. The clutch must be let in gradually, and without any sign of a jerk.

To engage second and third gears, the foregoing procedure is repeated, each time pushing (or pulling on some cars) the gear lever into the next notch. Gear-changing is something of an art on a veteran motor car, and though there is nothing in it—given a good gear-change mechanism—some time will elapse before the driver of a strange car will be able to change speed up and down without crashing or hit-and-miss methods. An hour's practice on a quiet country lane or a fairly level sports field will do more to teach the art of silent gear-changing than the most explicit written instructions. In "top" gear, the speed of the car can usually be varied between about 10 and 30 m.p.h. by only using the foot accelerator —only hills will require that the gear is changed.

The following somewhat humorous and sarcastic "Don'ts" for motoring novices was issued by the De Dion Company way back in 1913, but they are nevertheless golden rules which, if they were observed today, would make motoring a much more pleasant occupation:

Don't try to do with the horn and brakes what should be done with your head and the throttle.

Don't begrudge a good motor car a good supply of good oil, good petrol, good grease and clean water. Clean water costs nothing.

Don't look back after you pass a man in a car twice the size of yours. He may not like it, and there's generally something to watch ahead.

Don't rush ahead when you can't see ahead. "Ahead" is the place where collisions come from.

Don't drive fast around corners—it costs

a lot of rubber. Slow down, save money, and avert skidding.

Don't let the clutch in with a bang. It will—any clutch will. Rear tyres cost money too.

Don't crash-change gears. Handle the gear lever lightly; the gear-box will sort out the gear without force.

Don't insist on your share of the road. The other fellow may have the same idea. Even if you're in the right, he may be dangerous company. Give him all the room he wants.

Don't forget to light your lamps while you can see to read that it is time to light up.

Don't try to squeeze between two other vehicles—even if they are stationary. You may save ten seconds, but the record time for painting, varnishing and fitting a new mudguard is about four days.

Don't coin excuses to the policeman for the tail-lamp that blows out or shakes out. A decent rear-lamp costs about a guinea—a fine, 50s.

These few general hints are founded upon observation of all sorts and conditions of drivers [the pamphlet ends]. If you neither need nor appreciate such hints, pass them on to somebody who does.

Never steer a veteran car sharply from the side of the road into the centre, for it will usually slide its rear into the gutter. This applies particularly to a lightweight car. Should such a side-slip occur, do not touch the brakes or de-clutch, but ease down the engine speed and turn the front of the car in the same direction as the rear wheels have skidded. Incidentally, if gentle, easy motions of steering and gradual applications of clutch and brakes are made at all times, side-slips will be avoided on all but the very worst roads when they are wet.

In a veteran, the best performance will generally be got out of the engine by driving with the ignition as far "advanced" as possible without the engine "knocking". As much additional air as possible should be admitted to the mixture as is compatible with the speed of the engine and the tendency for it to misfire.

And, finally, a word of warning. Sometimes on wet grass or a really slippery hilly by-road the rear wheels will skid round under the power of the engine. Far more effective than pushing the car to help it to start is to pull on the top spokes of the front wheels. NEVER pull on the rear wheels, for should they spin round the person holding the spokes is at once liable to very serious injury.

All the foregoing hints are "veteran" hints applying to veteran cars, which should be driven as explained. Modern driving technique, of course, is entirely different—as are modern cars.

The National Motor Museum at Beaulieu

By now you will be asking, "Where can I see some veteran motor cars?"

Here is the answer to that question.

Some years ago, Lord Montagu of Beaulieu formed a special museum devoted to all forms of mechanical transport at his home, Beaulieu, which is situated in the midst of the beautiful New Forest. It was called the Montagu Motor Museum and was named after his father, who was one of the first motorists in Great Britain and had the honour of taking King Edward VII for one of his first motor rides.

The museum has now been renamed the National Motor Museum at Beaulieu and it houses approximately one hundred veteran and vintage cars as well as a collection of motor cycles, cycles, lorries, trams and some beautiful models and engines. There is also a special Racing Car Section which includes three world speed record-breaking cars, one of which is the famous *Golden Arrow*, which went at 231 m.p.h.

Thousands of people visit Beaulieu every year to see, not only the Motor Museum, but the famous Beaulieu Abbey and the house, which is Lord Montagu's ancestral home. Beaulieu is midway between Southampton and Bournemouth and the Montagu Motor Museum is open every day of the year. Make sure you pay a visit soon; it will be an unforgettable outing for you.

1914 Armstrong-Whitworth

List of Veteran Car Makes up to 1919

British makes, including Continental makes and those American makes which were commercially sold through agents in Britain

(With date of first production or mention)

1914 Talbot

Deemster 2-seater of 1919

Dodge 2-seater of 1919

Aberdonia	1912
A.B.C.	1918
A.C. (tricar)	1904
Ace	—
Achilles	1902
Achles-Turrell	1899
Adams	1907
Adams-Hewitt (later Adams) .	1906
Adamson	—
Ader	1904
Adler	1908
A.G.R.	1911
Airex	1907
Aisla Crag	1906
Ajax	1914
Albany-Lamplough (steam) .	1904
Albert	1918
Albion	1904
Albruna	1910
A.L.C.	1913
Alcyon . . .	1904 and 1912
Alda . . . . Only 1914
Alldays	1903
Alldays and Onions. *See* Traveller.	
Allsop	1904
Anderson	1918
Anglian	1903
Angus-Sanderson . . .	1918
Arden	1914
Argo	1916
Argyll (once Hozier) . .	1902
Ariel	1901
Aries	—
Arrol-Johnston . . .	1902
Armstrong-Siddeley . .	1919
Armstrong-Whitworth . .	1907
Ascot	1915
Astahl	1907
Aster . . Only 1909 and 1910
Atalanta	1916
Atholl	—
Austin	1906
Austro-Daimler . . .	1909
Autocar	1903
Autocrat	1913
Automixte (Peiper) . .	1907

Automobilette	1913
Averies–Ponette . . .	1913
Aviette ("Hurlingcar") . .	1915
Baby	—
Baguley	1912
Bailleau	1904
Ballot ("Cummicar") . .	1913
Bardon	1903
Barre	—
Barriere	—
Baudouin-Dechamp . .	1902
Bayard	1912
Beacon	—
Bean	1918
Beardmore	1918
Beaufort	1903
Bedelia	—
Bedford	1910
Bedford-Buick . . .	1916
Belgica	1901
Bell	—
Belsize	1900
Bentall	1907
Bentley	1918
Benz	1885
Benz-Parsifal . . .	—
Benz-Sohne	1912
Berkeley	—
Berliet	—
Bergman	1898
Bersey (electric) . . .	1897
Bianchi	—
Bifort	—
Bollée	1894
Bolide	1898
Boyer	1904
Bozier	—
B.R.	1916
Brasier	1906
Brenna	1911
Briscoe	—
Brit	—
Briton	1911
Britannia	1907

Brixia-Zust	. . . .	1916
Brooke	. . . .	1900
Brotherhood	. . . .	—
Brouhot (French)	. . .	1903
Brown	. . . .	1902
Brush	. . . .	1901
B.S.A.	. . . .	1908
Buchet	. . . .	1912
Buckingham	. . . .	—
Bugatti	. . . .	—
Buick	. . . .	1908
Butler (tricycle)	. . .	1885
Butterosi (French)	. .	1918
C. and H.	. . . .	1901
Cadillac	. . . .	—
Cadogen	. . . .	—
Calcott	. . . .	—
Calthorpe	. . . .	—
Cameron	. . . .	1912
Canterbury	. . . .	1903
C.A.R.	. . . .	1918
Carden	. . . .	—
Cassell	. . . .	1902
Century	. . . .	1900
C.G.V. (Charron)	. . .	1902
Charron (C.G.V.)	. . .	1902
Chalmers	. . . .	1908
Chambers	. . . .	1907
Chandler	. . . .	1918
Chenard-Walcker	. .	1903(c)
Chelmsford (steam)	. .	1902
Chevrolet	. . . .	1918
Cheswold	. . . .	—
Chater-Lea	. . . .	—
Chiribiri	. . . .	—
Chriton	. . . .	1903(c)
C.I.D.	. . . .	—
Citroen	. . . .	1918
Clement	. . . .	1900
Clement-Talbot	. . .	—
Clerk	. . . .	1895
C.L.C.	. . . .	—
Cluny	. . . .	—
Clyde	. . . .	1910(c)

Colibri	. . . .	1911
Coltman	. . . .	1909
Columbia	. . . .	1917
Coronet	. . . .	1901
Cottereau (of Dijon)	. .	1901
Cottin-Desgouttes	. .	1909
Cowey	. . . .	1911
Cote	. . . .	—
Courier	. . . .	—
Coventry-Precision	. .	—
Creanche	. . .	1904(c)
Cremorne	. . .	1901
Crescent	. . . .	—
Creouan	. . . .	1903
Crossley	. . . .	—
Crowden	. . . .	1899
Crowdy	. . . .	1911
Crouch	. . . .	1918
Croxted	. . . .	1903
Crypto	. . .	1904(c)
C.S.B. (Straker-Squire)	. .	—
Cupelle	. . . .	—
Cumbria	. . . .	—
Cummicar (Ballot)	. .	1913
Cyclone	. . . .	—
Daimler (Cannstadt)	. .	1885
Daimler (English)	. .	1899
Daimler-Mercedes	. .	1908
Darracq	. . . .	1901
Darracq-Bollée	. . .	1899
Davy	. . . .	1911
Dawson	. . . .	1918
Day-Leeds	. . . .	1918
Deasy	. . . .	1906
De Dietrich (Turcat-Méry)	. .	1899
De Dietrich-Bugatti	. .	—
Decauville	. . . .	1899
De Dion	. . . .	1895
De Dion Bouton	. . .	—
De Dion Corré	. . .	—
Deemster	. . . .	1918
Delage	. . . .	1909
Delahaye	. . . .	1895
Delauney-Belleville	. .	—

De La Vergne	. . . .	1895
Delta	. . . .	1904
Denis du Bois	. . .	1903
Dennis	. . . .	1910
Deschamps	. . .	1901
Detroiter	. . . .	—
De Boisse	. . .	1904
D.F.P.	. . . .	1910
Delamere-Deboutteville	. .	1903
Diatto	. . . .	1911
Dixi	. . . .	1906
De P.	. . . .	—
Dewcar	. . . .	—
D.L.	. . . .	—
D.M.C.	. . . .	—
Dodge	. . . .	—
Dodson	. . . .	1910
Dolphin	. . . .	1909
Dort	. . . .	—
Douglas	. . . .	1918
Dowsing (electric)	. .	1903
Drummond	. . .	1908
Ducroiset	. . .	1899
Duo	. . . .	—
Dufaux	. . . .	1904
Durkopp	. . .	1903
Durtea	. . . .`	—
Duryea	. . . .	1895
Duplex	. . . .	1918
Durnahot	. . .	1916
Eagle	. . . .	1903
Elburn-Ruby	. . Only	1911
Elmo	. . . .	1918
Elswick	. . . .	1902
E.M.F. (Studebaker)	. .	1912
Empire	. . . .	—
Empress	. . . .	—
Enfield-Allday	. . .	1918
Ensign	. . . .	1918
Excelsior	. . . .	1911
F.A.B.	. . . .	—
Fifnir	. . . .	1910

Farman	. . . .	1918
F.I.A.T.	. . . .	1910
F.I.F.	. . . .	—
Firefly	. . . .	1901
Fischer	. . . .	1904
Fergus	. . . .	
F.L.	. . . .	—
Flanders	. . . .	1912
Florentia	. . . .	1907
Florio	. . . .	—
F.N.	. . . .	1911
Ford	. . . .	1903
Forest	. . . .	1911
Forman	. . . .	1906
Forster	. . . .	1901
Foy Steele	. . .	—
Frenay	. . . .	—
Friedman	. . . .	1904
Gaggenau	. . . .	1906
Gamage	. . . .	—
Gardner-Serpollet	. .	1901
Gauthier-Wehrle	. .	1899
George Richard	. .	1899
Germaine	. . . .	1901
Gillet-Forest	. . .	1901
Gilyard	. . . .	—
Girling	. . . .	—
Gladiator	. . . .	1902
Globe	. . . .	—
G.M.C.	. . . .	1904(c)
G.N.	. . . .	—
Gobronne-Brillie	. .	1899
Goodchild	. . . .	—
Gordon	. . . .	—
Gnome	. . . .	—
G.R.	. . . .	—
Graham-White (buckboard)	.	1918
Gregoire-Campbell	. .	1918
Guy	. . . .	1918
G.W.K.	. . . .	1912
Hagen	. . . .	1904
Hallamshire	. . .	1902

Hampton	1918	Kendall	—
Hammond	1918	Kennedy	—
Hansa	—	King	1918
Hart (electric)	1903	Kitto	1903(c)
Hautier	1904	Knight of the Road	—
H.E.	1918	Knight-Junior	—
Henriod	1904	Koch	1904
Herald	—	K.R.I.T.	1912
Hermes	1903	Krupcar	1902
Heron	1906	Korte	1903(c)
Hillman	1908		
Hillman-Coatelen	—		
Hispano-Suiza	1908	La Buire	1907
H.L.	—	Lacoste	—
Hobson	1907	Lacre	1911
Holcar	1902	Lagonda (car)	1912
Horch	—	La Licorne	1911
Horley	—	Lambert-Herbert	—
Hornet	—	Lanchester	1899
Horbick	1902	Lancia	1908
Horstman	1918	La Ponette	—
Hotchkiss	—	Laurin-Klement	1908
Hozier (later Argyll)	—	Lawton	—
Hudson	1912	Leader	—
Humber	—	Leander	1904
Hupmobile	1911	L.E.C.	—
Hurlincar (Aviette)	1915	Le Gui	1911
Hurtu	1899	Leigeoise	1899
Hurtu (with Ariel)	1918	Leon Bollée	—
		Lewis	1895
		Lindsay	—
Iden	—	Little Midland	1918
Imperia	1909	L.M.	—
Invicta	—	Locomobile	1900
Iris	—	Londonia	—
Isotta-Fraschini	—	Loreley	1912
Itala	1911	Lorraine-Dietrich	—
		Lotis	1908
		Lozier	—
Jackson	1903	Lucar	—
James and Browne	1902	Luxior	—
J.B.S.	—		
Jennings	—		
Jowett	—	M.A.F.	—
J.P.	1908	Maja	1908
Junior	1907	Majola	

Macy-Roger	1895	Mueller-Benz 1895
Maibohm	1917	Munson (electric) . . 1903(*c*)
Malandin	1903	Mutel . . . . . —
Marca-Tre Spada . . .	—	
Marchand	1908	
Marathon	—	
Marlborough	1910	N.A.G. . . . . 1907(*c*)
Marshall-Aster . . .	—	Nagant-Hobson . . . —
Martini	1901	Nardini . . . . . —
Mass	—	Napier 1901
Mass-Paige	—	National 1904
Mascotte	1918	Nazzaro . . . . —
Mathis	—	N.B. 1911
Maudeslay	1901	N.E.C. 1911
Maxim	1901	Newey . . . . . —
Maxwell	1911	New Imperial . . . —
Matchless	—	New Hudson . . . —
Mees	1899	New Leader . . . . —
Medea	—	New Orleans . . . 1901
Mendip	—	New Pick . . . . —
Mercedes	—	Nelson 1904
Meredith	1904	Newton . . . . —
Merrall-Brown . . .	1919	Newton-Bennet . . . —
Metallurgique . . .	—	Niclausse . . . . —
Mercury	1918	Noe-Boyer . . . 1903
Meteorite	1918	Nordenfelt . . . 1907
Milde (electric) . . .	1903(*c*)	Norfolk 1904
Milnes } . . .	1903	Norma . . . . . —
Milnes-Daimler }		North British (Drummond) . —
Miesse	1908	Northern 1908
Minerva	1903	N.S.U. 1911
Mitchell	1911	N. and P. 1904
M.M.C.	1899	
Mobile	1902	
Monroe	—	Oakland . . . . —
Monarch	—	Ogston (Deemster) . . —
Mors	1899	Okodyne 1901
Morgan	—	Old Mill . . . . —
Morgan-Adler . . .	1918	Oldsmobile . . . 1901
Morris	1903(*c*)	Opel 1908
Morris Cowley . . .	—	Orleans . . . . —
Morris Oxford . . .	1913	Orient 1903
Motobloc	1908	Oryx 1911
Motorette	—	O.T.A.V. (Cupel) . . 1909
M.P.	1908	Overland 1911
M.S.L.	1911	Owen 1907

Packard	 1902	Renfrew 1903
Palmer	 1917	Renault 1899
Palladium	 1911	Reo . . . . . . —
Panhard	. . . . . —	Rex 1910
Panhard-Levassor	. . 1894	Rex-Remo 1909
Parr	 1901	Richard Brasier . . . 1904
Paragon	. . . . . —	Richardson 1903
Pascal	 1901	Riley 1907
Passey-Thellier	. . . 1903	Ritz . . . . . . —
Patton (electric)	. . . 1903	Rochet 1901
P.D.A.	. . . . . —	Rochet-Schneider . . . 1911
Pearson-Cox (steam)	. . —	Rolland-Pilain . . . 1918
Pelham	 1903	Rollo . . . . . —
Perry	. . . . . —	Rolls-Royce . . . . —
Peugeot	 1894	Roots 1899
Phanomobile	. . . 1911	Rothwell . . . . —
Phoenix	 1907	Rover . . . . . —
Piccard-Pictet	. . . 1908	Roydale 1908
Pick	 1902	Rugge . . . . . —
Pieper (petrol-electric)	. . 1903	Ruston-Hornby . . . 1918
Pierce-Arrow	. . . 1918	Royal Enfield . . . 1904(c)
Pilain	 1906	Roy 1904
Pilgrim	 1907	Ribble . . . . 1904(c)
Pilot	 1910	Ryknield . . . . 1902(c)
Pivot	. . . . . —	
Pony-Richard	. . . 1902	
Pope-Toledo	. . . 1904	Sabella . . . . . —
Portland	. . . . —	Salmon (Baguley) . . . —
Porthos	 1907	Sandringham . . . . —
P.M.C.	. . . . . —	S.A.V.A. . . . . . —
Premier	. . . . . —	Saxon 1918
Princess	. . . . . —	S.C.A.R. 1911
Prosper-Lambert	. . 1903(c)	S.C.A.T. 1907
Prunel	. . . 1904(c)	Schneider 1911
Pullman	 1911	Scout 1906
Pyramid	. . . . . —	Secqueville-Hoyau (Bugatti-designed) 1918
		Seabrook-R.M.C. . . . 1911
Radia	 1904	Service . . . . 1904(c)
Raleigh	. . . . . —	Serpollet . . . . —
Rambler	 1903	Shamrock 1908
Ranger	. . . . . —	Sheffield-Simplex . . . 1908
Rapid	 1907	Sherwyn . . . . . —
Regal	 1902	Siddeley 1906
Relyante	 1902	Siddeley-Deasy . . . 1910
Remo	 1908	Simms . . . 1901 and 1907

Six-cylinder engine of veteran Austin racing car

Four-cylinder engine of 25 h.p. Renault of 1912

*" Josephine "—the 1908 Renault
in the process of rebuilding and overhaul*

1910 Reo two-seater

Camping with a Ford Model " T " in 1918

Single-cylinder Rover out on army manoeuvres in the First World W.

*An early chauffeur-
driven Crossley*

*" Phoenix " two-seater
of the 1918 period*

1913 " *Humberette* " *light car*

1913 " *Bull-nosed* " *Morris two-seater*

" Josephine " on the road to Wales with the author and his son—its owner

38 h.p. Lanchester motor car of 1913

Simms-Welbeck	. . .	1902	Trumbull	1910
Simplicia	1911	Tribet	1911
Singer	—	Turcat-Méry (De Dietrich) . .	1899
Sirron	1911	Turicum	1910
Sizaire-Naudin . . .	1907	Turgan and Foy . . .	1904
Sizaire-Berwick . . .	—	Turner	1911
S.K.-Simplex . . .	1909	Turner-Miesse . . .	1907
Sloane	—	Turrel-Bollée . . .	1899
Soames	—	Tweenie	1914
S.P.A.	1909	Tylsley	—
Speedwell	1903		
Sperber	—		
Springuel	1911	Unic	—
Spyker	1902	Universal	—
Standard	1902		
Stanley (steam) . . .	1902		
Stella	1908	Val	—
Stellite	—	Valee	1899
Star	1902	Valveless	1908
Starling	1907	Vauxhall	1903
Stoddard	—	Varley Woods . . .	1918
Stoewer	1911	Velox	1912
Stoewer-Mathis . . .	1911	Vermorel	1911
Stoneleigh (Armstrong-Siddeley) .	1918	Vesta	1903
Stag	—	Via	1910
Straker-Squire . . .	1908	Victor	—
Studebaker	—	Vinot	—
Sturmey-Duryea . .	1903(c)	Vinot-Deguingand . .	1904
St. Vincent . . .	—	Violette	—
Sunbeam	1902	Vivinius	—
Super	—	Vox	—
Surridge	—	Vulcan	1902
Swift	1901	Vulpes	—
Talbot	—	Wall	—
Taunton	—	Warne	—
Thames	1908	Warren-Lambert . . .	—
Thor	1918	Wartburg	1903(c)
Thornycroft . . .	1901	Watsonia	1903(c)
Tiny	—	Waverley	1911
Toledo	1904	Weigel	1907
Tony-Huber . . .	1903	Weller	1904
Torbinia	1910	Werner	—
Torpedo	1909	West-Aster . . .	1907
Traveller (Alldays) . . .	1904	Western	1901

Westinghouse	.	.	.	.	1908
White (petrol)	.	.	.	.	1910
White (steam)	.	.	.	.	1901
Whitlock	.	.	.	.	—
Wilson-Pilcher	.	.	.	1900
Wilton	.	.	.	.	1918
Williamson	.	.	.	.	—
Wingfield	.	.	.	.	—
Winton	.	.	.	.	1899
Winco	.	.	.	.	—
Windhoff	.	.	.	.	—
Wolf	.	.	.	.	—

Wolseley	.	.	.	.	—
Wolseley-Siddeley	.	.	.	1910
Woodrow	.	.	.	.	—
Yaxa	.	.	.	.	—
Zebra	.	.	.	.	—
Zedel	.	.	.	.	1908
Zust	.	.	.	.	1907
Zephyr	.	.	.	.	1918

Studebaker open tourer of 1919

APPENDIX TWO

List of American Veteran Car Makes up to 1919

Including British and Continental makes marketed in the United States of America
(With date of first production or mention)

1914 Panhard

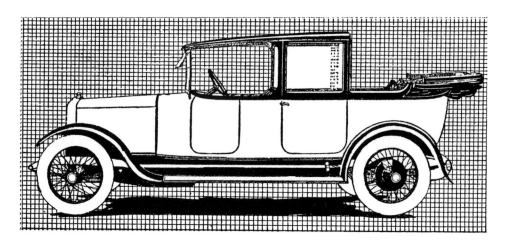

25 h.p. Coupé cabriolet of 1919

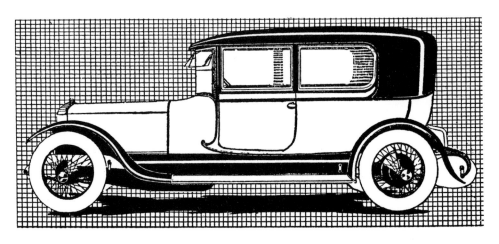

30 h.p. Daimler saloon of 1919

Abbott-Detroit 1912	Atlas (two-stroke) . . . 1907
A.B.C. 1906	Atlas-Knight 1911
Abendroth and Root . . . 1907	Atterbury 1911
Acason 1915	Auburn 1903
Acme 1903	Aultman (steam) . . . 1901
Adams 1904	Aurora 1906
Adams-Farwell (rotary rear engine) 1906	Austin 1914
Adrian 1902	Auto-Acetylene . . . 1899
Advance 1909	Autobug 1906
Aerocar 1905	Auto-dynamic 1901
Ajax . . . 1901 and 1914	Automobile Voiturette . . 1900
Akron 1901	Automotor 1901
Aland 1917	Auto Vehicle 1903
Albany 1907	
Alco 1909	
Alden-Sampson 1904	Babcock (electric) . . . 1906
Allen 1914	Bachelles 1901
Allen-Kingston 1907	Bailey (electric) . . . 1907
Alpena 1911	Baker (electric) . . . 1899
Alter 1916	Baker (steam) . . . 1917
American . . 1901, 1903 and 1910	Baldner 1901
American (electric) . . . 1902	Baldwin (steam) . . . 1900
American (steam) . . . 1903	Banker (electric) . . . 1905
American Beauty . . . 1917	Barnes . . . 1907 and 1912
American Berliet . . . 1909	Barrow (electric) . . . 1896
American Power Carriage . . 1900	Bartholemew (later "Glide") . 1901
American Underslung. . . 1915	Bates 1903
American Simplex . . . 1908	Bauer 1914
Ames 1912	Bay State 1906
Amplex 1910	Beacon 1908
Ams-Sterling 1917	Beardsley (electric) . . . 1901
Anchor 1909	Beau-Chamberlain . . . 1905
Anderson . . 1908 and 1915	Beggs 1918
Angus 1908	Belden 1907
Anhut 1909	Bell . . . 1907 and 1915
Apperson 1903	Bellefontaine 1907
Apple 1909	Belmont 1910
Apollo 1906	Bendix 1907
Arbenz 1914	Benham 1914
Ardsley 1905	Ben Hur 1917
Argo (electric) 1912	Benner 1908
Argo (petrol) 1914	Berg 1902
Argonne 1919	Bergdoll 1909
Ariel 1905	Berkshire 1905
Artzburger 1902	Bertolet 1908
Atlantic 1915	Bethlehem. 1908

Beverly	. . . . .	1904
Biddle	. . . . .	1915
Bimel	. . . .	1911
Binney-Burnham	. .	1902
Birch	. . . .	1918
Black Crow (later "Elkhart")	.	1908
Black Diamond	. . .	1904
Blackhawk	. . .	1903
Bliss (steam)	. . .	1906
B.L.M.	. . . .	1907
Blomstrom	. . .	1904
Blood	. . . .	1903
Boggs	. . . .	1903
Bolte	. . . .	1900
Borland (electric)	. .	1903
Borland-Granis	. .	1903
Boss (steam)	. . .	1903
Boston	. . . .	1900
Boston High-wheel	. .	1908
Bour-Davis	. . .	1915
Bournonville	. . .	1914
Bramwell	. . .	1902
Braisie	. . . .	1914
Brasier	. . . .	1903
Brecht (electric)	. .	1901
Breeze and Lawrence	. .	1905
Brennan	. . . .	1908
Brew and Hatcher	. .	1904
Brewster	. . . .	1917
Brewster-Knight	. .	1916
Brighton	. . . .	1914
Briscoe	. . . .	1914
Bristol	. . . .	1902
Broc	. . . .	1910
Brodesser	. . .	1914
Brown	. . . .	1916
Brownie	. . . .	1915
Browniekar	. . .	1908
Brunn	. . . .	1906
Brush	. . . .	1906
Bruss	. . . .	1907
Buckeye	. . . .	1901
Buckmobile	. . .	1903
Bucmobile	. . .	1907
Buffalo (electric)	. .	1900
Buffum	. . . .	1900

Buggycar	. . . . .	1909
Buick	. . . .	1904
Burdick	. . . .	1909
Burg	. . . .	1912
Burns	. . . .	1909
Bush	. . . .	1907
Byrider (electric)	. . .	1908
Cadillac	. . . .	1902
Cameron	. .	1903 and 1914
Campbell	. . . .	1917
Canda	. . . .	1900
Cannon	. . . .	1904
Cantono	. . . .	1905
Capitol (steam)	. . .	1902
Carhartt	. . . .	1911
Carlson	. . . .	1904
Carnation	. . . .	1912
Carrol	. . . .	1914
Cartercar	. . . .	1907
Cartone	. . . .	1905
Case	. . . .	1910
Cato	. . . .	1907
Centaur (electric)	. . .	1902
Central	. . . .	1905
Century (petrol)	. . .	1900
Century (electric and steam)	.	1901
C.F.	. . . .	1908
Chadwick	. .	1905 and 1911
Chalfont	. . . .	1906
Chalmers	. . . .	1908
Champion	. . . .	1909
Chandler	. . . .	1913
Chapman (electric)	. . .	1901
Chase	. . . .	1907
Chelsea	. . . .	1901
Chevrolet	. . . .	1912
Chicago (petrol)	. . .	1899
Chicago (steam)	. . .	1906
Chicago (electric)	. . .	1913
Chief	. . . .	1908
Chino	. . . .	1909
Christie (front wheel drive)	.	1904
Christopher	. . . .	1908
Church	. . . .	1902

Churchfield (electric) . . . 1913	Covert 1901
Cincinnati (steam) . . . 1903	C.P. 1908
Clark (steam) 1900	Craig-Toledo . . . 1906
Clark (electric) . . . 1906	Crane 1912
Clark-Carter 1900	Crane and Breed . . . 1912
Clark-Hartfield 1908	Crawford (Dagmar) . . . 1905
Clarkmobile 1902	Crescent . . . 1905 and 1906
Classic 1917	Crest 1903
Clear and Dunham . . . 1908	Crestmobile 1901
Clendon 1908	Cricket . . . . . 1914¯
Clermont (steam) . . . 1903	Crompton 1905
Cleveland 1902	Crowdus (electric) . . . 1901
Cleveland (Chandler's) . . 1919	Crow-Elkhart 1911
Cloughley 1902	Crown High-wheel . . . 1907
Coates-Goshen . . . 1908	Crouch (steam) 1900
Coey 1911	Crowther 1915
Colburn 1907	Crowther-Duryea . . . 1917*
Colby 1911	Croxton (ex-Keeton) . . 1909
Cole 1909	Cruiser (camping car) . . 1918
Collings (electric) . . . 1901	Cucmobile 1907
Colt 1908	Culver 1905
Columbia 1900	Cunningham (steam) . . . 1901
Columbia-Knight . . . 1916	Cunningham (petrol) . . . 1912
Columbus (electric) . . . 1902	Cutting 1909
Columbus (petrol) . . . 1903	C.V.I. 1907
Comet 1917	
Commonwealth . . . 1917	
Compound 1904	Dalton 1911
Conover 1907	Daniels 1915
Conrad (steam) . . . 1900	Darby 1909
Conrad (petrol) 1904	Darling . . . 1901 and 1917
Continental . . 1907 and 1914	Darrow 1903
Cook 1907	Dart 1914
Coppack 1907	Davenport 1902
Corbin 1903	Davis 1910
Corbitt 1911	Dawson 1904
Cornelian 1914	Dayton (electric) . . . 1915
Cornish-Friedberg . . . 1904	Deal 1908
Correja 1908	Decker 1901
Cort 1914	Deere 1906
Corwin 1905	Deering Magnetic . . . 1919
Cosmopolitan . . . 1907	De Kalb 1915
Cotta (steam) 1901	De la Vergne 1895
Country Club . . . 1904	De Luxe 1906
Courier . . . 1904 and 1909	De Mats 1905
Courier-Clermont . . . 1912	De Mot 1909

De Motte 1904	Eclipse (steam) . . . 1901
Derain 1911	Economy . . . 1906 and 1917
Desberon 1901	Eddy (electric) 1902
De Shaw 1906	Edwards-Knight . . . 1913
De Soto 1913	Elcar 1909
De Tamble 1909	Elco 1914
Detroit . . . 1900 and 1912	Eldredge 1903
Detroit-Chatham . . . 1912	Electra (electric) . . . 1915
Detroit-Dearborn . . . 1909	Electrobat (front wheel drive) . 1895
Detroit Electric 1907	Elgin . . . 1900 and 1916
Detroiter 1913	Elite (steam) 1901
Dewabout 1899	Elk 1914
Diamond . . 1905 and 1907	Elkhart 1908
Dile 1914	Elliot 1902
Disbrow 1917	Ellis 1901
Dispatch 1911	Elmore 1901
Dispatch Valveless . . . 1915	Elwell-Parker (electric) . . 1910
Dixie . . . 1908 and 1916	Emancipator 1909
Doble (steam) 1913	Emerson 1917
Dodge 1914	E.M.F. 1909
Dodo 1909	Empire . . 1898 and 1914
Dolson 1904	Empire State . . . 1901
Dorris 1902	Enger 1909
Dort 1915	Entyre 1911
Douglas 1918	Erie 1919
Dowagiac 1908	Essex (steam) . . . 1901
Dragon 1906	Essex (petrol) 1906
Drexel 1917	Essex (Hudson-built) . . 1917
Drummond 1916	Euclid 1907
Duck 1911	Eureka 1907
Duer 1907	Evansville 1907
Dumont 1904	Everitt 1909
Dunn 1914	Everybody's . . . 1908
Duplex 1909	Ewing 1908
Duquesne . . . 1903 and 1912	Excelsior 1899
Durocar 1907	
Duryea 1895	
Dyke 1902	Fageol (cars) . . . 1917
	Fairmount . . . 1906
	Falcar 1909
Eagle (electric) 1912	Falcon . . 1909 and 1914
Eagle Rotary 1917	Famous 1909
Earl 1907	Fanning 1902
Eastman (steam and petrol) . 1899	Farmac 1915
Easton 1907	Federal (steam) . . . 1906
Eck 1903	Federal (petrol) . . . 1908

Firestone-Columbus . . .	1907	Gramm-Logan	1908
Fischer . . .	1902 and 1914	Grant	1913
Flanders (electric) . . .	1911	Grant-Ferris . . .	1901
Flint	1902	Great Arrow (Pierce-made) .	1904
Ford	1903	Great Eagle . . .	1911
Forest City (later Jewel) . .	1906	Great Smith . . .	1907
Fort Pitt	1908	Great Southern . . .	1910
Foster (steam and electric) .	1898	Great Western . . .	1908
Fostoria	1906	Greeley . . .	1903
Fournier	1902	Greuter	1899
Franklin (air-cooled) . .	1902	Gride	1903
Frayer-Miller . . .	1904	Grinnell . . .	1915
Fredonia	1902	Griswold . . .	1907
Friedman	1900	Grout (steam) . . .	1896
Fritchie (electric) . .	1907	Gurley . . .	1900
Frontenac . . .	1909	Guy-Vaughan . . .	1912
F.R.P.	1915	G.V. . . .	1906
Fuller	1908	Gyroscope (Blomstrom) . .	1904
Fulton	1908		
F.W.D. (4-wheel drive and steering)	1910		
		Hackett	1915
		H.A.L. (previously Lozier) .	1916
Gaeth (steam and electric) . .	1898	Hall	1903
Gale	1904	Halladay . . .	1908 and 1918
Galt	1915	Halsey	1901
Gardner	1919	Hamilton . . .	1917
Garford	1907	Hanson	1918
Gas-au-Lac . . .	1905	Hardy (made by Flint) . .	1902
Gasmobile . . .	1900	Harper	1907
Gayford	1911	Harrison . . .	1904
Gearless . . .	1907	Harroun . . .	1916
G.E.C. (steam and electric) .	1898	Hartford (electric) . .	1895
Gem	1917	Hart-Kraft . . .	1908
General	1903	Harvard . . .	1915
Genesee	1911	Hasbrouck . . .	1899
Geneva (steam) . . .	1901	Hassler . . .	1917
Geronimo . . .	1918	Hatfield . .	1906 and 1917
Ghent	1917	Havers . . .	1908
Gibbs (electric) . . .	1904	Hawley . . .	1907
Gifford-Pettitt . . .	1907	Hayberg . . .	1907
G.J.G.	1909	Haydock . . .	1907
Gleason	1910	Haynes . . .	1900
Glide	1903	Haynes-Apperson . .	1895
Grabowsky . . .	1908	Hayward . . .	1913
Graham	1903	Hazard . . .	1914
Graham-Fox . . .	1903	Hebb	1918

Heine-Velox	1908	I.H.C. (Harvester) . . .	1899
Henderson	1912	Interstate	1908
Henley (steam) . . .	1899	Intrepid	1904
Henry	1911	Iowa	1908
Herff-Brooks . . .	1915	Iroquois	1903
Herreshoff . . .	1909		
Herschel-Spillman . .	1905		
Hertel	1895	Jackson . . 1899 and 1902	
Hess (steam) . . .	1902	James	1911
Hewitt	1905	Janney	1906
Hewitt-Lindstrom . .	1900	Jarvis-Huntingdon . .	1912
Heyman	1905	Jaxon (steam) . . .	1903
Hill	1907	Jay	1907
Hillsdale . . .	1908	J.I.C.	1913
Hobby Accessible . .	1909	Jeannin	1908
Hoffman (steam) . .	1901	Jeffery (later Nash) . .	1914
Hoffman (petrol) . .	1903	Jenkins	1907
Holland	1905	Jewel (later Keeton) . .	1906
Holley	1902	Jewett	1906
Hollier	1916	Johnson (steam). . .	1905
Homes	1918	Jones	1915
Holsman (buggy) . .	1905	Jones-Corbin . . .	1902
Holyoke	1899	Jonz	1908
Homer	1908	Jordan	1916
Homer-Laughlin . .	1916		
Houghton . . .	1904		
Houpt-Rockwell . .	1909	Kane-Pennington (British design) .	1894
House (steam) . . .	1901	Kansas City . . .	1905
Howard (steam) . .	1901	Karbach . . .	1908
Howard (petrol) . 1903 and 1913		Kauffman . . .	1909
Hudson (steam) . .	1901	Kearns	1908
Hudson (petrol) . .	1909	Keeton (later Croxton) .	1908
Huffman	1916	Kenmore	1909
Huntingdon . . .	1907	Kensington (steam and electric) .	1899
Hupmobile . . .	1908	Kent	1917
Hupp-Yeats (electric) .	1911	Kermath	1908
Hydromotor . . .	1917	Kerns	1915
		Keystone (steam) . .	1901
		Kiblinger . . .	1907
Ideal . . 1904 and 1908		Kidder (steam) . . .	1900
Illinois (electric) . .	1897	King	1905
Illinois (petrol) . .	1909	Kinnear	1917
Imperial (petrol) . .	1900	Kirk	1903
Imperial (electric) . .	1907	Kissel (ex-Kisselkar) . .	1906
Ingrame-Hatch . .	1917	Kline Kar . . .	1909
International . . 1900 and 1901		Klink	1905

Klonk	. . . .	1900
Knickerbocker	. . .	1901
Knox	. . . .	1900
Knox-Lansden	. . .	1904
Kobusch	. . .	1906
Koehler	. . . .	1910
Konigslow	. . .	1903
K.R.I.T.	. . .	1911
Krock	. . . .	1904
Kunz	. . . .	1902
Laconia	. . . .	1900
Lambert	. .	1904 and 1908
Lancamobile	. . .	1900
Lane (steam)	. . .	1899
Lansden (electric)	. .	1915
Lanphier	. . .	1909
La Petite	. . .	1905
La Salle-Niagara	. .	1906
Laughlin	. . .	1914
Laurel	. . .	1917
Lauth-Juergens	. .	1907
Law	. . . .	1902
Leach	. . . .	1899
Leader	. . . .	1911
Lear	. . . .	1900
Lebanon	. . .	1906
Lenox	. . . .	1912
Lewis	. . . .	1898
Lewis (later Hollier)	. .	1913
Lexington (ex-Howard)	.	1908
Liberty	. . . .	1916
Lincoln	. . . .	1908
Lion	. . . .	1907
Little	. . . .	1912
Locomobile (steam and petrol)	.	1899
Logan	. . . .	1905
Lone Star	. . .	1917
Loomis	. . . .	1900
Lorraine	. . . .	1907
Lozier (later H.A.L.)	. .	1901
Luedinghaus-Espenschied	.	1919
Luverne	. . .	1906
Lyman	. .	1904 and 1909
Lyman-Burnham	. .	1903

Lyons	. . . .	1911
Lyons-Atlas	. . .	1912
Lyons-Knight	. . .	1914
Maccar	. . .	1906
McCrea	. . .	1906
McCue	. . .	1909
McFarlan	. . .	1912
McIntyre	. . .	1909
McLaughlin	. . .	1916
Mackle-Thompson	. .	1903
Macon	. . .	1917
Macy	. . .	1895
Madison	. . .	1915
Mahoning	. . .	1904
Maibohm	. . .	1916
Majestic	. . .	1917
Malcolm	. . .	1915
Malvern	. . .	1905
Manhattan	. . .	1905
Marathon	. . .	1909
Marble-Swift	. .	1903
Marion (made by Willys)	.	1910
Marion-Handley	. .	1916
Marlboro (steam)	. .	1900
Marmon	. . .	1903
Marquette	. . .	1912
Marr	. . .	1903
Marsh (steam)	. .	1898
Marsh (petrol)	. .	1914
Marshall	. . .	1919
Martin-Wasp	. .	1919
Marvel	. . .	1906
Maryland	. . .	1906
Mason	. .	1906 and 1908
Massachusetts	. .	1901
Master	. . .	1918
Matheson	. . .	1903
Mathews	. . .	1907
Maumee	. . .	1906
Maxim-Goodridge (electric)	.	1908
Maxwell (later Chrysler)	.	1910
Maxwell-Briscoe (later Maxwell)	.	1904
Mead	. . .	1912
Mecca	. . .	1915

Media . . . 1900 and 1907	Mulford 1909
Meiselbach 1904	Multiplex 1914
Mercer 1910	Muncie 1906
Mercury . . 1904, 1914 and 1918	Murdaugh 1900
Merkel 1905	Murray 1918
Messerer 1901	
Meteor (steam) . . . 1902	
Meteor . . 1904, 1914 and 1918	Nance 1904
Metz (*ex*-Waltham) . . . 1909	Napoleon 1919
Metzger 1909	Nash 1917
Michigan 1903	National (electric and petrol) . 1900
Midgley 1905	Neftel (electric) . . . 1903
Midland 1908	Neilson 1907
Mier 1908	Nelson 1905
Mighty Michigan . . . 1911	Neustadt-Perry . . . 1903
Milburn (electric) . . . 1915	New England Steam . . . 1900
Milwaukee (steam) . . . 1900	New England Electric . . 1900
Minneapolis 1914	New Era (built by Moon) . . 1916
Mitchell 1903	New Home 1901
Mitchell-Lewis 1902	New Parry 1911
Mobile (steam) . . . 1899	New Pittsburg . . . 1915
Model 1903	New York 1909
Modern 1907	Niagara . . 1903, 1904 and 1916
Mohawk 1903	Noma 1919
Mohler 1901	Norma 1916
Moline . . . 1904 and 1911	Northern 1903
Moline-Knight (later R. and V.) . 1914	Northwestern . . . 1904
Monarch . . 1905, 1907 and 1914	Norton 1901
Moncrief 1901	Norwalk 1912
Mondex-Magic . . . 1914	Nyberg 1912
Monitor . . 1909 and 1915	
Monroe 1915	
Moon 1905	Oakland (later Pontiac) . . 1907
Moore . . 1902 and 1916	Oakman 1898
Mora 1906	Ofeldt (steam) . . . 1899
Moreland (cars) . . . 1919	Ogren 1916
Morgan 1910	Ohio (electric) . . . 1900
Morriss-London (built for British	Ohio (petrol) . . . 1909
market) 1919	Okay 1907
Morse (steam) . . . 1904	Okey 1903
Morse (petrol) . . . 1915	Oldsmobile 1898
Motorette 1911	Oliver 1905
M.P.M. 1914	Olympian 1917
Mover 1902	Omaha 1912
Moyea 1902	Ophir (steam) . . . 1901
Moyer 1911	Oregon 1916

Orient (steam)	1900	Pierce 1909
Ormond (steam) . . .	1904	Pierce-Arrow 1901
Orson	1911	Pilgrim 1914
Otto	1909	Pilliod 1916
Ottokar	1903	Pilot 1909
Overland (built Willys) . .	1903	Pioneer 1909
Overman (steam) . . .	1899	Pittsburg (electric) . . 1896
Owen	1910	Pittsburg (petrol) . . 1909
Owen Magnetic . . .	1915	Planche 1906
Owen-Schoeneck . . .	1914	Plymouth 1909
Oxford (steam)	1900	Pomeroy 1902
Oxford (petrol)	1905	Ponder 1916
		Pontiac 1902
		Pope-Hartford . . . 1895
Pacific	1904	Pope-Toledo . . . 1901
Packard	1899	Pope-Tribune 1904
Page	1906	Pope-Waverley 1904
Page-Toledo	1910	Porter . . . 1900 and 1919
Paige	1909	Portland 1914
Palmer	1906	Postal 1907
Palmer-Singer . . .	1907	Powercar 1909
Pan	1918	Pratt 1912
Pan-American . . 1901 and 1917		Premier (electric gear-change) . 1903
Panther	1909	Prescott (steam) . . . 1901
Paragon	1906	Primo 1911
Parry	1911	Princess . . 1905 and 1914
Parsons	1905	Pullman 1906
Partin-Palmer . . .	1914	Pungs-Finch 1904
Paterson	1908	
Pathfinder	1913	
Pawtucket	1901	**Q**ueen 1905
Payne-Modern . . .	1907	Quick 1900
Peerless	1900	Quinian 1904
Penn	1911	
Pennsy	1917	
Pennsylvania (steam) . . .	1905	**R**.C.H. 1912
Pennsylvania (petrol) . . .	1907	Rainier . . 1905 and 1911
People's	1901	Rambler (later Jeffery and Nash) . 1903
Perfection	1906	Randall (steam) . . . 1903
Perfex	1912	Randolph . . . 1910
Petrel	1908	Ranger 1907
Phelps	1902	Rapid 1903
Phianna	1905	Rassler 1907
Phoenix	1900	Rauch and Lang (electric) . . 1905
Pickard	1911	Rayfield 1911
Piedmont	1918	Read 1913

Reading (steam)	.	.	.	1901	Santos-Dumont .	.	.	.	1902
Reber	.	.	.	1902	Saxon	.	.	.	.	1914
Red Jacket	.	.	1911	Sayers	.	.	.	.	1917
Reeves	.	.	.	1911	Schacht (cars)	.	.	.	1904
Regal	.	.	.	1908	Schaum	.	.	.	.	1905
Regas	.	.	.	1903	Schnader .	.	.	.	1907
Reid	.	.	.	1903	Scripps-Booth	.	.	.	1904
Reliable	.	.	.	1906	Searchmont	.	.	.	1900
Reliable-Dayton	.	.	1909	Sears-Roebuck	.	.	.	1907
Reliance .	.	.	.	1903	Sebring	.	.	.	.	1909
Remington	.	.	.	1901	Selden	.	.	.	.	1907
Reo (R. E. Olds of Oldsmobile) .	1904	Sellers	.	.	.	.	1909
Republic .	.	.	.	1915	Senator	.	.	.	.	1906
Revere	.	.	.	1918	Seneca	.	.	.	.	1917
Rhodes	.	.	.	1908	S.G.V. (electric gear-change)	.	1910
Richard	.	.	.	1917	Shadwick	.	.	.	1917
Richmond.	.	.	.	1908	Shain	.	.	.	.	1902
Ricketts	.	.	.	1909	Sharp-Arrow	.	.	.	1909
Riddle	.	.	.	1916	Shatswell .	.	.	.	1905
Rider-Lewis	.	.	.	1908	Shawmut	.	.	.	1905
Rigs-that-Run	.	.	.	1899	Shaw-Wick	.	.	.	1904
Riker (electric and petrol) .	1898	Shelby	.	.	.	.	1902
Roader	.	.	.	1911	Shoemaker	.	.	.	1907
Roamer	.	.	.	1916	Sibley-Curtis	.	.	.	1906
Roberts	.	.	.	1904	Signet	.	.	.	.	1913
Robinson	.	.	.	1900	Silent	.	.	.	.	1902
Rock Falls	.	.	.	1919	Silver Knight	.	.	.	1906
Rodgers	.	.	.	1903	Simons (steam)	.	.	.	1898
Roebling .	.	.	.	1909	Simplex	.	.	.	.	1907
Rogers	.	.	.	1911	Simplex-Crane .	.	.	1918
Rogers and Hanford .	.	1901	Simplicity	.	.	.	1907
Roman	.	.	.	1909	Singer	.	.	.	.	1916
Ross (steam)	.	.	.	1905	Single-centre	.	.	.	1907
Ross (petrol)	.	.	.	1916	Sintz	.	.	.	.	1903
Rotary (Bournonville)	.	1914	S.J.R.	.	.	.	.	1915
Royal Tourist	.	.	1904	Skene (steam)	.	.	.	1900
Russell	.	.	.	1903	Smith	.	.	.	.	1905
					Smith and Mabley Simplex	.	1901
					Sommer	.	.	.	.	1905
Saginaw	.	.	.	1914	Soules	.	.	.	.	1905
St. Joe	.	.	.	1909	Spacke (cycle car)	.	.	1919
St. Louis (Rigs-that-Run)	.	1899	Spaulding	.	.	.	1900
Salisbury (electric)	.	.	1896	Speedway	.	.	.	1904
Salter	.	.	.	1909	Speedwell	.	.	.	1907
Sampson .	.	.	.	1904	Sphynx	.	.	.	.	1915
Sandusky	.	.	.	1903	Spiller	.	.	.	.	1900

Spoerer	. . . .	1909
Springer	. . . .	1904
Springfield (steam)	. . .	1900
Springfield (electric)	. .	1908
S.S.E.	. . . .	1917
Stafford	. . . .	1911
Stammobile (steam)	. .	1905
Standard (petrol)	. . .	1902
Standard (electric)	. .	1915
Standard (petrol)	. . .	1916
Stanhope	. . . .	1899
Stanley (steam)	. . .	1895
Star	. . . .	1903
States	. . . .	1918
Staver	. . . .	1907
Steamobile	. . .	1901
Stearns (steam)	. . .	1898
Stearns (petrol)	. . .	1900
Stearns-Knight	. . .	1917
Steel Swallow	. . .	1907
Steinway (piano firm)	. .	1895
Stephens	. . . .	1916
Sterling	. . . .	1909
Sternberg	. . . .	1909
Stetson	. . . .	1917
Stevens-Duryea	. . .	1902
Stewart	. . . .	1916
Still (electric)	. . .	1901
Stilson	. . . .	1908
Stoddart-Dayton	. . .	1904
Stoddart-Knight	. .	1911
Storch (steam)	. . .	1902
Strathmore (steam)	. .	1900
Stratton	. . . .	1909
Streator	. . . .	1905
Stringer (steam)	. . .	1901
Strong and Rogers	. .	1900
Struss	. . . .	1897
Studebaker (electric)	. .	1902
Studebaker (petrol)	. .	1902
Sturges (electric)	. .	1895
Stutz	. . . .	1913
Stuyvesant	. . .	1911
Suburban	. . . .	1912
Success	. . . .	1906
Sultan	. . . .	1908

Sun	. . . .	1918
Sunset (steam)	. . .	1901
Synnestvedt (steam)	. .	1904
Syracuse	. . . .	1905
Taunton	. . . .	1901
Templar	. . . .	1918
Temple	. . . .	1899
Templeton-Dubrie	. .	1910
Texan	. . . .	1919
Thomas	. . . .	1902
Thomas-Detroit	. .	1907
Thompson	. . .	1907
Thomson	. . . .	1900
Tincher	. . . .	1903
Toledo (steam)	. . .	1900
Toledo (petrol)	. .	1903 and 1909
Toquet	. . . .	1905
Torbenson	. . .	1905
Touraine	. . . .	1914
Tourist	. . . .	1903
Trebert	. . . .	1907
Triangle	. . . .	1917
Tribune	. . . .	1913
Tri-Moto	. . . .	1896
Triumph	. .	1900 and 1911
Trumbull	. . . .	1914
Tulsa	. . . .	1917
Twentieth Century	. .	1900
Twombly (steam)	. .	1904
Twombly (petrol)	. .	1913
Twyford	. . . .	1902
Union	. .	1902 and 1908
United	. . . .	1905
University	. . .	1907
Upton	. . . .	1902
U.S.	. . . .	1908
U.S. Long Distance	. .	1900
Van	. . . .	1909
Vandergraft	. . .	1907
Van Dyke	. . .	1912

Vaughan . . . 1905 and 1914	Westcott 1912
Velie 1908	Westinghouse 1901
Vernon 1915	Weston (steam) 1896
Viceroy 1915	Weston (petrol) . . . 1906
Victor (steam) . . . 1907	Whaley-Henriette . . . 1900
Viking 1908	White (steam and petrol) . . 1900
Virginian 1911	White (petrol) . . . 1909
Vixen 1914	Whiting 1905
Vogue 1918	Whiting-Grant . . . 1911
Vulcan 1913	Whitney (steam) . . . 1898
	Wildman 1902
	Willard 1905
Waco 1915	Willys 1917
Wagenhais 1914	Willys-Overland . . . 1908
Wahl 1914	Willys-Knight . . . 1914
Walker (electric) . . 1905	Wilson 1903
Wall 1901	Winton (with self-starter) . . 1896
Walter 1906	Wisconsin 1899
Waltham 1900	Wolf 1907
Walther 1903	Wolverine 1904
Walworth 1905	Wonder 1909
Ward-Leonard (electric) . . 1901	Woods 1900
Warren 1905	Woods Dual Power (petrol-electric) 1916
Warren-Detroit . . . 1909	Woods-Mobilette . . . 1915
Warwick 1901	
Washington . . 1907 and 1909	
Waterloo 1904	**Y**ale . . . 1903 and 1917
Waterous 1905	York 1905
Watt 1910	
Waverley . . . 1903	
Wayne 1904	**Z**entmobile 1903
Welch (overhead camshaft) . 1904	Zimmerman 1908